Help! My College Students Can't Read

Help! My College Students Can't Read

Teaching Vital Reading Strategies in the Content Areas

Amelia Leighton Gamel

ROWMAN & LITTLEFIELD
Lanham • Boulder • New York • London

Published by Rowman & Littlefield
A wholly owned subsidiary of
The Rowman & Littlefield Publishing Group, Inc.
4501 Forbes Boulevard, Suite 200, Lanham, Maryland 20706
www.rowman.com

Unit A, Whitacre Mews, 26-34 Stannary Street, London SE11 4AB

British Library Cataloguing in Publication Information Available

Library of Congress Cataloging-in-Publication Data is available on file.

ISBN 978-1-4758-1456-9
ISBN 978-1-4758-1457-6 (paperback)
ISBN 978-1-4758-1458-3 (ebook)

∞™ The paper used in this publication meets the minimum requirements of
American National Standard for Information Sciences—Permanence of Paper
for Printed Library Materials, ANSI/NISO Z39.48-1992.

Printed in the United States of America

For my sons, Kyle and Eric, who first inspired me to teach.

Contents

Acknowledgments

The idea to write this book arose out of a deep desire to equip content-area faculty who desperately wanted to help the struggling readers in their classes. I would conduct workshop after workshop and do dozens of classroom demonstrations and walk away knowing the instructors I worked with still needed something that I couldn't supply.

They needed an easy-to-use guide filled with simple yet workable ways to embed reading strategies into their college classes in the shortest amount of time possible and with the least amount of preparation. When I could not find such a guide for them, I began to dream about creating one myself.

I really had no idea what a big project this dream would turn out to be. I also did not realize how many wonderful people would help me bring it to reality. Without them this book could never have been written.

It is with deep appreciation that I first want to thank the numerous content-area instructors, who despite their genuine need to protect every moment of their limited teaching time to cover content, have supported my work, welcomed me into their classes, and embraced the idea of taking time to share the application of reading strategies using their course texts and materials. Special thanks to Mary Belknap, Mark Schopmeyer, and Ted Miller.

I owe a great debt of gratitude to Charlotte Finnegan as well. Her tireless work and passion for higher education undergirds everything I do as an educator.

I would also like to thank the hundreds and hundreds of students who have allowed me to work with them as they were learning, practicing, and taking in feedback about their experiences applying reading strategies across content areas.

Special thanks to the reviewers who took time to read and critique chapters: Jenny Schanker, Susan Gabriel, Paige Eagan, and Linda Fleischer.

I would like to thank the professionals who, amid their full and demanding schedules, took time to be interviewed about the demands of reading in their fields: Brian Amsden, Pamela Asti, Jason Brinker, Shenita Brokenburr, Monique Caston, Sherry Chiasson, Scott Costa, Thomas Gonda, Judith Josiah-Martin, Don Murphy Jr., Kenneth Seel, Mark Sutherland, and Gilbert Perez III.

Many thanks to Rowman & Littlefield Publishing for taking a chance on a new author.

My sincere thanks to Kimberly Cutting, simply put, the most true and loyal friend there ever was, for her constant support and encouragement.

To my husband, Kiernan, to whom I offer my deepest gratitude for cups of tea, continuous support, encouraging texts, and reminders of my passion for education and student success. I will be forever grateful he finally found his way to me.

My deepest and most sincere thanks to Rhonda Hurst for her expertise, organization, advice, creativity, kindness, patience, friendship, and tireless commitment to this book. As I walked into an undergrad writing class many years ago, there was no way I could have known that my instructor would one day provide countless hours of editing for my first book. But I am so grateful it turned out that way.

Introduction

The first week of classes has just ended. I gather my reading students' papers, a hard copy textbook, and an e-device and put them into my bag. While walking across campus to my office, I think about Liam, who has attended every day so far but brings nothing with him other than his cell phone, which he uses compulsively to send text messages. While unlocking my office door, I mull over reasons struggling readers are often so disconnected from what's going on in the classroom—apathy, fear, shame, defeat.

I drop my bag, log on, and check my inbox when I notice an e-mail from a psychology instructor:

Friday, September 7
Help! My students can't read!
Jack

Some might think an e-mail like this would bring a college reading specialist like me a lot of frustration. Not so. In fact, it's quite the opposite. Jack's e-mail fills me with hope. He is one of so many instructors I have come across who know their students are drowning, but who desperately want to throw them a life ring. I quickly fire off a response.

Friday, September 7
When can we have a meeting? Is tomorrow too soon?
Amy

Jack's e-mail clearly illustrates the frustration he and so many other content-area faculty experience with the growing numbers of Liams in their classes. There is bountiful research to indicate that students are leaving high school underprepared for college work. At one college where I collected data, nearly 80 percent of entering freshmen needed at least one developmental course. Over 40 percent were reading between seventh- and twelfth-grade levels and were placed in reading classes.

Traditionally such classes have been the remediation strategy of choice for most colleges and universities. Students take one to two semesters of developmental reading and then move on to regular content-area courses like economics or psychology. However, most students cannot leap two to six reading levels in one or even two semesters. A great number of them are still not ready for the challenges of academic reading in spite of taking and passing developmental classes.

This will come as no surprise to content-area instructors like Jack. They are keenly aware of the reading deficits of the students in their courses. They are also aware that more often than not their institutions are looking to them as the second line of defense even when they have no specialization in the area of reading.

This is not likely to change any time soon. As a matter of fact, it is likely to get worse. As a way to deal with ballooning budgets, some colleges and universities are cutting developmental education programs or eliminating them altogether. Students who come into college with below-level reading abilities are being sent straight into non-developmental classes with little or no remediation.

These students are not the only ones who need help with the challenges of academic reading. Technology is making it difficult for even average or above-average readers to navigate college-level texts. The current generation of readers is becoming more and more accustomed to short pieces of information and to quickly clicking away that information if it is not interesting or is difficult to understand. Old-school methods of opening a book and reading it cover to cover have been abandoned. Students, even relatively strong readers, now need strategies to be able to identify and glean only the most relevant information from texts in the shortest amount of time and to be able to understand, to retain, and to use that information.

The reality in colleges today is that students need to be taught reading skills in *all* of their classes. And their teachers know this. In workshop after workshop, I hear the same frustrations over and over. The Jacks (and the Jills) feel trapped because they don't know how to help and they don't have time to help. "We're not trained reading instructors," they say. "And we have hundreds of students and too much material to cover already." Legitimate points.

Content-area instructors need solid, simple reading strategies that can be taught to their students without compromising the integrity of their courses or reducing the amount of time spent on content material. And they are not only reaching out to reading specialists for help with this. They are reaching for books that address the reading problems they are encountering in their classrooms.

In my experience trying to help these instructors, I have not found a book that specifically attends to the needs of college students who read at high school (or even middle school) levels. Nor have I found one that offers reading strategies and activities designed especially for college-level content-area texts. For the reading classes I teach, I had to purchase resources published for secondary teachers. While these materials realistically addressed my students' reading levels and provided activities to increase their skills, they were often inadequate because of the strong middle school and high school focus.

Help! My College Students Can't Read is designed to fill that gap. The goal of this book is to equip instructors to teach their students active reading strategies without compromising the integrity of their courses and without adding a lot of extra work. Such strategies will help students know how to successfully navigate their way through content-area texts and to engage with the material in them. Active, engaged readers are more able to comprehend information and to remember and use that information.

Many students do not have any idea what it means to be an active reader. When they hear about it in a college classroom, the concept will be brand new to them. Others will have some idea and maybe even some experience, but it will not be something they intentionally practice, especially with academic texts. For this reason, chapter one provides an explanation of how instructors can introduce active reading to their students. Also included is a detailed description of how to model the process in a way that will give students some initial experience with several reading strategies. This will help prepare them to learn about each strategy in more detail later on.

Chapters two through seven each focus on a specific reading strategy with detailed explanations and examples to help instructors teach that particular strategy to students. These chapters are not in any special order that represents a sequence in which the strategies should be taught. Instructors can choose the best time to teach a specific strategy to suit the needs of their content area and course objectives.

Chapter eight, the final chapter, more thoroughly addresses the "how much time will this really take" question and offers further suggestions about how to teach reading strategies in the content areas in the most effective ways.

Most chapters also have other special features. One is called "Professional Spotlight." This contains a photo of a professional person, the person's job title, and an interview that highlights how vital reading with comprehension is to someone in that particular field. The purpose is to give instructors evidence they can use to show students that knowing how to read well is not just a skill they need to get a college diploma, but is a skill they need to be successful in their chosen careers.

Another feature is called the "Toolbox." It offers a variety of teaching ideas and resources directly related to the strategy discussed in the particular chapter. Some are general and can be applied to any content area and some are more content specific. This feature is designed to give instructors ideas they can readily use in their classrooms without a lot of time and energy searching for resources on their own.

The final feature is called "Putting It to Work." This section provides a more detailed lesson or classroom activity. Again, some are general and some are more content specific. However, all can be adapted to fit nearly any subject area.

The content in each chapter is not only based on current best practice in the field of reading, but on over fifteen years of professional experience. As a college reading instructor and a campus-wide reading specialist, I have not only worked with students but with hundreds of administrators and instructors demonstrating the application of reading strategies in content-area classrooms and facilitating strategy-specific and content-specific reading workshops. Before becoming a full-time faculty member, I served as a college administrator, leader of college student success initiatives, adjunct instructor, teacher trainer, educational presenter, and public school teacher.

Many different aspects of my work inspired me to write this book, but none more than my deep desire to help students be successful readers and to help their dedicated content-area instructors who want this as much as I do.

Active Reading

Tell me and I forget, teach me and I may remember, involve me and I learn.

—Benjamin Franklin

Professional Spotlight

Figure 1.1.

It's not just about reading, it's about thoroughly understanding what's being read and being able to take that and apply it to new policies that can be created to make changes federally. If a person can't read, comprehend, and apply it to current day situations, they would definitely experience some challenges.

Monique Caston,
Senior Manager of Special Programs

Chapter 1
Reasonable question: How can I improve students' reading abilities without sacrificing valuable time?

Successful readers are active readers. They don't just mechanically read words, letting them glide through their minds like a stock exchange ticker tape. Instead, they engage with those words, they interact with them, they infuse them with meaning based on their understanding of the world, and they digest them to nourish that understanding. Many readers instinctively learn this as they gain experience, but the unfortunate reality is that many do not. For this second group, active reading is a skill they need to be taught, especially as they face the challenges of college-level texts.

Hurst and Pearman, from Missouri State University, point out specific strategies used by proficient readers, such as predicting, rereading, visualizing, making connections, and using context clues. These strategies can be effectively taught. It takes those who know the skills to teach them to those who do not.

As instructors, we are much further down the road in our reading skills than most of our students. This is especially true when reading in our content areas. We can help move our students toward this kind of expertise by modeling how we think through a text. When the strategies are taught, learned, and applied, they can make a big difference. Instead of just seeing and saying the words and coming away from the text empty-handed, students will have a greater chance of comprehending the material and really learning it.

The best way to teach this skill is by example. According to Handy and Stein (2010), research indicates that, as human beings, we are designed to learn by imitating what we see others do. Modeling reading strategies for students helps them learn to think through what they are reading and to make connections to enhance comprehension (p. 23). In other words, students need to see the active reading process in action and then be guided along as they practice it themselves.

If we only tell our students how to be active readers, they won't remember or have a frame of reference on which to draw later. They need to hear *and* see us in action when working through a text. They need to see how we handle unknown words, jot down notes, create visuals, ask questions, and search for answers. Then they need to be involved in doing those things themselves with us there to lead and guide. The good news is that this doesn't take as much time and work as one might think.

Consider this example. Imagine a master baker offers to teach you how he makes his award-winning piecrusts. He wouldn't help you very much if he just gave you general instructions ("Mix flour, shortening, and water in a bowl."), then expected you to fill in the blanks. Instead, you would benefit the most if he explained the steps in detail ("Measure out 2½ cups of organic flour."), showed you how to follow them ("Watch me as I use this pastry cutter to 'cut' in the shortening."), and involved you in the process ("Here's a pastry cutter for you. Let's do it together.").

This wouldn't take hours and hours of time and preparation. It would just take the master baker being willing to walk you through a process that he knows well.

You can teach your students to be active readers in the same way. Simply put, tell your students, show your students, and involve your students.

The rest of this chapter will explain ways to go about this, provide detailed descriptions of active reading demonstrations that include a wide variety of strategies, list ideas and activities that can be readily applied in any classroom, and offer sample lessons for particular content areas.

Subsequent chapters will focus in detail on teaching specific reading strategies and helping students decide how to choose which ones work best in different contexts. For example, making inferences to think through a piece of literature, constructing visual images to understand concepts in biology or earth science, and making connections between familiar and unfamiliar information to comprehend processes in automotive, technology, or health occupations.

MODELING ACTIVE READING IN THE CLASSROOM

Before students learn to choose specific strategies, they need an overall demonstration of active reading to introduce them to the concept and to let them see how much more effective and efficient their reading can be.

In such an active reading demonstration, the instructor will display a piece of text at the front of the class, then work through the process with the students. A video of such a demonstration can be viewed at www .youtube.com/watch?v=mGO5L8-ome4.

Instructors can start teaching active reading at any point during a semester; however, it is usually best to begin as early as possible. The sooner students learn active reading strategies, the sooner they can put them to use. Also, as with any type of teaching and learning, repetition is key. Starting early gives students more time to practice these new skills under the guidance of their instructors. Ideally, active reading should be introduced during the first or second week of class and then revisited several times throughout the term to reinforce learned strategies and to introduce new ones.

The piece of reading used in the demonstration can be a selection from a textbook or an excerpt from an article or essay. It can also be a more creative piece, such as the short fictional story, "The Cough," by Harry Humes, which is used in the video demonstration mentioned earlier and will be used as an extended example in this chapter. A creative text does not necessarily have to be related to an instructor's content area, but very well could be. For example, selections from Barbara Kingsolver's work could be used in biology, ecology, or sociology classes.

Using short fiction, whether related to the content area or not, can be very effective to present active reading strategies. Many students are familiar with fiction and can usually understand the message of the content with little difficulty. Once students see how strategies are applied with familiar fictional material, transferring the strategies to more difficult or unfamiliar texts will be easier.

The length of the demonstration piece is another thing to consider. To be effective, it should be around one page of double-spaced type. A text that is too short will not allow students to see a variety of active reading strategies. A text that is too long can overwhelm them and make the process seem daunting. The ideal piece should provide just enough text to adequately model reading strategies and keep students engaged.

In the appendix is a list of sources for good content area articles, the full text of "The Cough," and a "quick start" guide for doing a classroom demonstration of active reading. The titles of a few other fictional gems can be found in the Toolbox.

To see how an active reading demonstration works, let's look into the classroom of an instructor we will call Julian, who will be using "The Cough." Julian will start by putting the text on a document camera.

Each student will be given a copy of the story, but not at first. This will allow Julian to control how much of the text his students see at the beginning of the activity. Having the text displayed on the doc cam during the demonstration will also enable students to see how their instructor works his way through the active reading process.

Vygotsky's philosophy of people learning best from other people is the premise for the kind of modeling Julian will be doing. Students who are fortunate enough to observe instructors navigating texts, making connections between concepts, and wrestling with new and unknown theories have an enormous advantage. They are being taught not only how to take in the information as they read but how to process it as well. Seeing an expert wade through material and demonstrate how to analyze, evaluate, and learn from it gives students a much greater chance of being able to replicate the process.

Julian will begin his demonstration with only the title showing. Students need to know that good readers read titles and predict, or guess, what the text might be about. Offering a sample guess will help them get started. Julian points to the title, "The Cough," and says, "Hmm . . . when I read the words 'The Cough,' I think of a smoker's cough. This makes me wonder if the text will be about a smoker who coughs." Then he writes "smoker's cough" on the text near the title.

Depending on the type of technology instructors are using, annotations can be handwritten or typed using annotation features. It is good for students to see this done both ways since some will have hard copies of reading material and others will have e-texts.

Teaching students to write their thoughts, ideas, and questions as they read is important. Simply writing things down helps students to focus their attention on what they are reading and to more effectively remember details later. Jotting down questions can signal that more information is needed from another source, such as an ancillary text, classmates, or the instructor. Annotating a text also allows students to revisit concepts and quickly review key material before quizzes or tests without rereading multiple times.

As Julian shows his thinking, he invites students to join in. "What other predictions could we make about the text based on the title, 'The Cough'?"

A mother of a toddler says, "It makes me think of whooping cough or croup."

In a typical active reading demonstration, some students, like this one, will respond readily. Others will be more hesitant. It is important to resist the urge to rescue them from their silence. Instead, provide adequate wait-time for response. Sometimes students simply need to think a bit more.

Other times, they have ideas but are afraid to voice them because they don't want to be "wrong."

This is especially true when students are asked to make predictions as they read. To ease these fears, remind them that it is not important for their predictions to be correct. It's only important that they make them. Psychologist Bluma Zeigarnik has written about what is called the Zeigarnik Effect. This is basically the idea that if you give your mind a task, it will work hard to complete it (Konnikova 2012). Arie Kruglanski, another psychologist, calls this a "Need for Closure." This need, Kruglanski says, "motivates us to work harder, to work better, and to work to completion" (as cited in Konnikova 2012).

When it comes to reading, our brains are wired to find the information we want to know. Making predictions before we read will give our brains something to look for, a purpose for reading. Then we can determine if our guesses are on target or if the text takes us in another direction.

Another way to create a purpose for reading is to ask questions about the possible content of the text. Julian asks, "Who has the cough?"

Then he solicits other questions from students (What's causing the cough? How serious is it?) and jots these in the margins also. These questions, along with the predictions about the title, will provide students with a focused purpose for reading—to search for answers and to find out if their predictions are correct.

On a side note, consider using text spelling in the jotted notes. For instance, the two questions from Julian's students could be written down like this: whts czing the cough? how srs is it?

Text spelling is a widely used form of modern-day shorthand that students know well. As actual shorthand was used by stenographers to save time, text-spelling is commonly used by students to save time. It will be a great advantage to them if we encourage it for note-taking in our classrooms.

Concerns that students will misuse this type of writing can be addressed by simply explaining when it is appropriate and when it is not. Just as stenographers understood that shorthand was not appropriate for formal business writing, students will understand that their "shorthand" is not appropriate for formal academic writing. Being allowed to use a honed skill like text spelling will help students be much more effective note-takers as they learn to actively read, with the added benefit that they are likely to find the process more enjoyable.

Once students have been shown how to make predictions and develop a purpose, they can be given copies of the story, either hard copies or pre-uploaded electronic versions they can access on their e-devices. Students can then be asked to mark up their copies as the class moves through each paragraph.

Students will tend at first to just copy what they see the instructor writing. That's okay. However, encourage them to also write thoughts of their own even if they don't share them with the class. Copying the instructor's notes is often the first step in learning how to annotate a text. As students add their own thoughts and ideas, instructors can provide feedback to help them recognize accurate inferences, link information, clarify ideas, or identify and process difficult concepts.

Once students have their copies, reveal the first sentence or two of the text on the doc cam, read the words aloud, and then think them through with the class. Julian reads the first sentence of "The Cough": *Our young father walked Ash Alley whistling, "Rescue the Perishing," but already he carried mine tunnels home in his black-streaked breath.* Julian stops there and points to the first few words, "Our young father." Then he asks, "Who is telling this story?"

A student responds, "A man's child."

"And what makes you think so?" Julian prompts.

The student pauses for a second, making sure what he thinks is correct. "It has to be the man's child because it says 'Our father.'"

"Exactly. And is there more than one child in the family?"

"Yes," says the same student. "Because it says our father, not my father."

On the text, near the words "Our young father," Julian jots down, "One of the children is telling the story."

This is an example of how an instructor can point out ways to think beyond the mere surface of a text. Julian's students might not have realized how important it can be to think about narrators, other characters, etc., while reading fiction. Talking through a text with an instructor demonstrates this type of intentional thinking.

Julian continues by underlining the words "Ash Alley" because he thinks they are important. Many students often mistakenly assume that everything in a text must be important and feel overwhelmed with the task of wading through it. Instructors can model how to be more discerning by pointing out what they see as important and explaining why they think so.

Julian tells his students, "I don't know where Ash Alley is or even if it's a real place, but I know what an alley is and what it looks like. I can see it, visualize it in my mind. In fact, in my mind it's dark because an ashy place would be dark."

Then Julian points to the words *"Rescue the Perishing"* and says, "I'm not familiar with that song, but the title reminds me of a church song, perhaps a hymn." This type of comparison shows students how to make connections between known and unknown things as they read. Connecting prior knowledge to new information is a well-known strategy that enhances comprehension and cements learning.

Next Julian is going to use a strategy called "word swapping." One reason academic texts seem challenging for students to read is because the vocabulary is often out of reach. Even if words are known but not a part of a student's everyday talk, they can inhibit reading fluency and interrupt comprehension. Word-swapping helps students replace less familiar words with more familiar ones. This simple strategy converts texts written with higher-level vocabulary and academic language to a level that is more easily understood.

Julian says, "I know what 'rescue' and 'perishing' mean, but I wouldn't use those words in my everyday talk. I'm going to swap them for words that I might say to help me better understand. What word means the same as 'rescue'?"

A student hesitantly suggests, "Save?"

"Great, that will work." Julian crosses out "rescue" and writes "save" above it. Then he inquires again, "What word could I use instead of 'perishing'? What does 'perishing' mean?"

Another student suggests, "Dying."

"I like it," Julian says. "I would definitely use the word 'dying' in my everyday talk instead of 'perishing.'" Then he crosses out the word "perishing" and writes "dying" above it. "Now let's read what we have so far," he says, "to hear how it sounds using our everyday talk." Then he reads aloud,

Our young father walked Ash Alley whistling, R̶e̶s̶c̶u̶e̶ the P̶e̶r̶i̶s̶h̶i̶n̶g̶. (Save / Dying)

"Quite an odd song for someone so young to be whistling," Julian says. "Perhaps it's a clue or foreshadowing of what is to come."

Then he reads again, *but already he carried mine tunnels home in his black-streaked breath.* Julian underlines the words "mine tunnels" and "black-streaked breath." Then he says, "I realize now that this man isn't a smoker, nor does he have a cold or croup. He is a coal miner."

A student says, "I'll bet he has black lung."

"Good guess. Tell me about that. What do you know about black lung?"

A bit hesitant now, the student says, "Well, I don't know a lot. But I think that when men work in the coal mines, they get black lung from all the dust. I think it's like lung cancer."

Often students think they know something, such as a definition, concept, or formula, but have difficulty when asked to explain it. When they are encouraged to elaborate and given time to talk through their thoughts, they can come to more understanding and clarity.

Julian continues through the text, reading and thinking aloud, helping students make connections. At one point, he reads the following lines: *My mother would look at him, her lips a line of impatience and fear. "Your lungs will soon be stone," she said.* To which the father replies, *"It's good money, Dorse. It's our only money."*

Julian takes a bit more time here because he realizes he has an opportunity to teach about inferences. "An inference is a conclusion we draw not based on something actually stated, but on what is implied or on our own understanding of similar situations," he says. Then he points to the name "Dorse" and asks, "Who is this?"

Without hesitation, several students say, "His wife."

"Right," Julian says. "The text doesn't specifically say this, but we can infer it because of the situation we are reading about and our own basic understanding of family dynamics during the time in which the story is set."

Then he asks, "I am going to infer also that the father doesn't really like his job. Why would I say this?"

The students are silent for a moment, and then one says, "Because he's doing it for the money."

"How do you know that?" Julian asks.

"Because he knows she doesn't like his job and he defends it by saying the money is good."

"Great answer," Julian says. "It wasn't something directly stated in the story. You inferred it."

Julian continues on through the text, reading about how the cough affected the family. When he comes to the line, *In the winter, it trailed behind my father like a peacock feather on a woman's hat,* he shows students how to use visual images to remember important points as they read. In the margin, Julian sketches a large brimmed hat with a long peacock feather trailing behind it, and he writes, "No matter where he goes, it's there."

Visual images are remembered images. The human brain takes in, interprets, and remembers images more quickly than it does text. Research has shown that the part of the brain wired for images is quite large. As a result, we can remember information much easier through visual cues than we can through verbal cues. Also, since visual images are concrete, unlike words, which are abstract, they are easier to remember (Kouyoumdjian 2012).

With another passage, Julian has an opportunity to show students what to do when they encounter unfamiliar vocabulary. He reads, *One summer he told us we were on a planet going nowhere fast. He made a model he called an orrery, and showed us how the heavens worked.* Julian asks, "What's an orrery?"

When no one answers, Julian has a student Google it on her phone. They quickly discover that an orrery is a model of the solar system powered by a clock mechanism. Julian also takes the opportunity to talk about context clues. "If you run into an unfamiliar word and don't have a way to look it up," Julian says, "there are a lot of strategies to try to figure out the meaning. One is to use context clues. That means you look at how the word is used in the sentence and at other words nearby with which you are familiar."

He points to the word "orrery" again in the text. "What nearby words could have helped us here?"

The students look at the passage for a moment. Then one volunteers, "He says it's a model of how the heavens work."

"Right," Julian says. "Some of us probably made models of the solar system when we were in school, so maybe we could relate to that. Even if we didn't, we've all probably seen one."

Another student says, "He uses the word 'planet' too."

"Yes," Julian says. "That word really helps us get a more clear idea of what 'orrery' might mean."

After Julian has worked through the whole text with the class, he leads a discussion about active reading. His students are surprised at how well they connected with Hume's story. They connected because they did what studies say skilled readers do and not what less-skilled readers do. They interacted with the text using effective reading strategies instead of just passively reading and rereading with few strategies beyond simple underlining (Di Tommaso).

In demonstrations like the one Julian used, students seldom have trouble seeing how effective such active reading can be, but they often worry about the time it will take. "Yeah, I can understand better," they say. "But I don't want to do this every time I have to read. It will take too long."

These comments are honest and accurate. It *would* take forever to move this slowly through each piece of text. The good news is that not every reading strategy needs to be so intentionally applied to everything a student reads. For instance, when students are reading familiar texts, with familiar content and vocabulary, they might not use very many strategies, and the ones they do use will be nearly automatic, like making connections, asking questions, searching for answers, and so on. However, more difficult texts require more intentional use of a wider variety of reading strategies.

Students who are in high school or in their first or second semesters of college are very likely to encounter more challenging reading. It is especially common for students transitioning to college to have difficulties with reading comprehension, and the need to provide students with concrete strategies for approaching reading tasks is well documented (Di Tommaso).

The University of Michigan's website page, "Strategies to Use While You Are Reading," gives students two types of reading strategies, elaboration (marking the text, drawing pictures, etc.) and organizational (concept maps, outlines, etc.). The intention is not that every strategy listed should be applied each time a text is read, but that students should know how to apply each strategy when they need it.

Another reason that students might not need multiple strategies every time they read is some strategies just aren't applicable to certain types of texts. For example, although opportunities to develop inferences abound in science when creating hypotheses and predicting outcomes, that isn't necessarily the case when reading science textbooks. Most inferences have been completed during the scientific process long before these books are written.

However, such texts do provide prime opportunities to restate information, to record questions, and to create visuals or concept maps. Students need to be taught a variety of strategies to be more successful with many types of reading. Teachers can then help students focus on the strategies that work best in their content area.

Although students do not need to so carefully and intentionally work through every reading task like Julian did "The Cough," they do need their teachers to demonstrate such careful and intentional work. And they need their teachers to give them opportunities to practice their new skills and to show evidence that they have learned them. In other words, we need to hold them accountable for using reading strategies in our classrooms.

When this topic comes up in workshops, a look of dismay appears on the faces of the instructors in the room. "How much time will *that* take?" the look says. Part of the answer is that no matter how much time it takes, it will be time well spent because students who can more effectively *read* the course material will more effectively *learn* the course material.

To accomplish this, we must not only teach them reading strategies but also require them to show "proof of doing." This phrase comes from Brockton High School in Massachusetts, which has gone from a failing school to a leader in school-wide literacy. Part of their strategy is to mandate that students show evidence of the skills they are learning (M. Connors, personal communication, October 28, 2013).

Holding students accountable for this "proof of doing" doesn't have to take as much time as one might think. In fact, it can take as little as ten minutes. In the appendix is a resource called "Take Ten." It is a list of reading activities with easy accountability that can be embedded in any content-area classroom in ten minutes or less.

THE BOTTOM LINE

If we teach our students how to read actively, give them time to practice those skills, and hold them accountable for doing so, they will be more engaged with the course material, remember more from it, and be more able to use what they have learned. It's a win-win. Instructors have deeper thinking students and students are more successful in their classes.

Remember the master baker teaching you how to make piecrust? Imagine that happened a few years and a few pies ago. Now when faced with the task, you have the measurements down pat and you're a whiz with a pastry cutter. And you got that way by being given instruction, being shown what to do, and being involved in doing it yourself. That's how, with our help, students will learn to be active readers.

TOOLBOX

- Ask student volunteers to demonstrate their thinking with a piece of text and their annotations on the doc cam.
- Ask another content-area instructor to read and mark up a short piece of text, then use it as an example in your classroom, so students can see how other people think as they read.
- Let students practice active reading in groups of four. This exercise helps students learn to annotate a text and lets them see how their peers think and make connections as they read. Choose a section of text and enlarge it to 11 × 17 (one copy for each group). Tape copies to the center of poster-sized pieces of paper, large enough to give students ample room to write comments. Hang these in several spots around the classroom. Assign one group to each poster. Give group members different colored markers and have them sign their names on the poster, so the work of each student can be identified. Have groups silently read and annotate their copy of the text with their thoughts, questions, visuals, connections, etc. Walk around and annotate with the students to model your thinking and to keep students on task. When they all seem finished, have students silently visit each group's text and write comments about their classmates' annotations, offer possible answers to their questions, etc. Then have students go back to their text and read their classmates' responses. End with a short class discussion of what students took away from this exercise.
- Show an active reading video demonstration: www.youtube.com/watch?v=mGO5L8-ome4 or www.youtube.com/watch?v=VUWNFqcYsto.

- Upload videos of your own classroom demonstrations to YouTube, so students can access them when needed or so you can use them in class as a quick reminder.
- Access high-interest texts or excerpts for active reading demonstrations from the list in the appendix and from the following sources:

English/Literature/Writing

"Celebration of the Human Voice," Eduardo Galeano
The Glass Castle, Jeanette Walls
The House on Mango Street, Sandra Cisneros
Maud Martha, Gwendolyn Brooks
"Salvation," Langston Hughes
"The Witness," John Edgar Wideman

Education/History/Criminal Justice/Political Science/Psychology/Sociology

Arc of Justice: A Saga of Race, Civil Rights, and Murder in the Jazz Age, Kevin Boyle
"Ballot or the Bullet," Malcolm X
"Black Men and Public Space," Brent Staples
"Civil Disobedience," Henry David Thoreau
Common Sense, Thomas Payne
"The Gettysburg Address," Abraham Lincoln
"In the Combat Zone," Leslie Marmon Silko
"Inaugural Address," John F. Kennedy
"Letter from Birmingham Jail," Martin Luther King Jr.
"The Meaning of July Fourth for the Negro," Frederick Douglass
"A Modest Proposal," Jonathan Swift
The New Jim Crow: Mass Incarceration in the Age of Colorblindness, Michelle Alexander
"Pearl Harbor Address to the Nation," Franklin D. Roosevelt
The Souls of Black Folks, W. E. B. Du Bois
There Are No Children Here: The Story of Two Boys Growing Up in the Other America, Alex Kotlowitz
The Warmth of Other Suns: The Epic Story of America's Great Migration, Isabel Wilkerson

Math/Science

The Amazing Life of Henrietta Lacks, Rebecca Skloot
A Brief History of Time, Stephen Hawking
The Curious Incident of the Dog in the Night-Time, Mark Haddon
Genome: the Autobiography of a Species in 23 Chapters, Matt Ridley
The Origin of Species, Charles Darwin
A Short History of Nearly Everything, Bill Bryson
Your Inner Fish: A Journey into the 3.5-Billion-Year History of the Human Body,
  Neil Shubin

PUTTING IT TO WORK

Below is an excerpt from chapter five of *The New Jim Crow*: *Mass Incarceration in the Age of Colorblindness* by Michelle Alexander. This is an ideal contemporary text to use for an active reading demonstration in a variety of content areas, such as political science, history, English, and criminal justice. Following the excerpt is a description of how you might go about using it with your classes.

Excerpt from chapter five of *The New Jim Crow: Mass Incarceration in the Age of Colorblindness* by Michelle Alexander

More African American adults are under correctional control today—in prison or jail, on probation or parole—than were enslaved in 1850, a decade before the Civil War began. The mass incarceration of people of color is a big part of the reason that a black child born today is less likely to be raised by both parents than a black child born in slavery. The absence of black fathers from families across America is not simply a function of laziness, immaturity, or too much time watching Sports Center. Thousands of black men have disappeared into prisons and jails, locked away for drug crimes that are largely ignored when committed by whites.

The clock has been turned back on racial progress in America, though scarcely anyone seems to notice. All eyes are fixed on people like Barack Obama and Oprah Winfrey, who have defied the odds and risen to power, fame, and fortune. For those left behind, especially those within prison walls, the celebration of racial triumph in America must seem a tad premature. More black men are imprisoned today than at any other moment in our history. More are disenfranchised today than in 1870, the year the Fifteenth Amendment was ratified prohibiting laws that explicitly deny the right to vote on the basis of race. Young black men today may be just as likely to suffer discrimination in employment, housing, public benefits, and jury service as a black man in the Jim Crow era—discrimination that is perfectly legal, because it is based on one's criminal record.

This is the new normal, the new racial equilibrium.

The launching of the War on Drugs and the initial construction of the new system required the expenditure of tremendous political initiative and resources. Media campaigns were waged; politicians blasted "soft" judges and enacted harsh sentencing laws; poor people of color were vilified. The system now, however, requires very little maintenance or justification. In fact, if you are white and middle class, you might not even realize the drug war is still going on. Most high school and college students today have no recollection of the political and media frenzy surrounding the drug war in the early years. They were young children when the war was declared, or not even born yet. Crack is out; terrorism is in.

Today the political fanfare and the vehement, racialized rhetoric regarding crime and drugs are no longer necessary. Mass incarceration has been normalized, and all the racial stereotypes and assumptions that gave rise to the system are now embraced (or at least internalized) by people of all colors, from all walks of life, and in every major political party. We may wonder aloud "where have the black men gone?" but deep down we already know. It is simply taken for granted that, in cities like Baltimore and Chicago, the vast majority of young black men are currently under the control of the criminal justice system or branded criminals for life. This extraordinary circumstance—unheard of in the rest of the world—is treated here in America as a basic fact of life, as normal as separate water fountains were just half a century ago.

During this activity, you will have an opportunity to guide your students through the following reading strategies. This list can be printed out and given to students after the demonstration to help them review what they have learned.

- Before reading, determine prior knowledge about the topic of the text.
- Predict what the text might be about.

- Determine a purpose for reading (what you want to know or what the author wants you to know).
- Underline and note important phrases or sentences.
- Utilize strategies for determining unknown words.
- Develop and record relevant connections to the text.

Start with a brief discussion of the book from which this excerpt is taken. Point out the title, *The New Jim Crow: Mass Incarceration in the Age of Colorblindness*. Model your thinking aloud for students by briefly sharing what you know about historical Jim Crow laws. Then point out the words "incarceration" and "colorblindness" and let students help define them. As you share, jot some of your thoughts and theirs in the margins near the title.

Then read the title of the excerpt and the first sentence and guide students to some predictions about what might be meant by "The New Jim Crow" and what they think the excerpt will be about. Jot these thoughts down as well. Briefly point out that predictions give us a purpose for reading (to find out if our predictions are correct) and help keep us focused as we read.

Explain that another way to determine a purpose for reading is to ask two questions: What do I want to know about this topic? What might the author want me to know? Lead students in a short discussion of these questions and briefly record their ideas.

Begin reading the excerpt aloud. As you go, show students how to underline sentences they think might be important and how to include a brief note describing why. For example, you could underline the second sentence in paragraph one: "<u>The mass incarceration of people of color is a big part of the reason that a black child born today is less likely to be raised by both parents than a black child born in slavery</u>."

Next to this, you could include a note that says, "Prison causes more single-parent families than slavery." Explain that simply underlining or highlighting without annotating does little to help us understand and remember what we are reading.

As you continue to read, point out words you have anticipated ahead of time that might be unfamiliar to students (disenfranchised, expenditure, racialized, rhetoric, etc.) Provide strategies they might use to determine unknown words if an e-device like a cell phone isn't available.

Such strategies could include looking at the words surrounding the unfamiliar word for context clues, guessing what the word might be and rereading the sentence swapping the word with their guess to see if it makes sense, determining if there is any part of the word they already know, or if it looks like or sounds like another word with which they are familiar.

Sometimes, as instructors, it is easy to forget that students often do not have the background knowledge that we do to support their understanding of what they are reading. During an active reading demonstration, it is important to put ourselves in the shoes of our students and anticipate areas where they might have difficulty. As you move through the text, briefly supply political or historical information where needed and anticipate and record questions students might be wondering about. As you do this, you can help students make connections with the prior knowledge they do have.

It is also very effective to help students make connections to their personal lives and to what they know from media sources, such as movies, television, the news, and the Internet. You can help them by sharing some of your own such connections and then inviting them to share theirs.

It is also effective to point out phrases or concepts you think are powerful, such as "Crack is out; terrorism is in" and explain why this struck you. This helps students learn how to go beyond the surface level of a text and to think more deeply as they read.

As you continue with this active reading demonstration, remember the goal isn't to apply every reading strategy you can think of. The goal is to teach students a limited number of strategies at a time to help them to construct meaning and to remember the information so it can be used later. Giving them too much at once can be overwhelming and even discouraging. Additional strategies can be taught later in other demonstrations throughout the semester.

To wrap up this activity, give students the list of reading strategies and guide them in a quick review of how each was used in the demonstration.

PROFESSIONAL SPOTLIGHT READING INTERVIEW WITH MONIQUE CASTON, MSW

Title: Senior Manager of Special Programs at Chicago Housing Authority
Location: Chicago, Illinois

Amelia: Could you take a moment and describe the types of reading required in your profession?

Monique: A lot of reading entails federal policies and federal regulations as it relates back to my day-to-day activities within my particular role. And then additionally for myself to stay abreast of my profession, I take the initiative to read various articles that relate to nonprofit management, management in general and also self-sufficiency.

Amelia: When you're reading those types of things, are you reading books, articles, or mainly looking at small chunks of information? What's the length involved?

Monique: I'm reading mostly articles and then small chunks.

Amelia: When you're reading an article, let's say a policy, do you read it word for word? Do you scan it or skip parts? How do you approach that?

Monique: Depending on the length, if it's short, maybe five to seven pages, then I will go ahead and read the entire thing. However, if I find it's very heavy with governmental words or phrases that I'm not really familiar with, I skim based upon specifically what I'm looking for first.

Amelia: How often do you read in your job?

Monique: I am definitely reading policies and regulations every day.

Amelia: You are obviously a proficient reader. How did you get that way? Did you have a good elementary school experience or was reading something that was valued in your home?

Monique: Definitely that's something that was valued in my home. As far as my education up until college, I went to all Chicago public schools for elementary school and for high school as well. My high school was one of the best in the city. However, my elementary school was the complete opposite. We were always on academic probation. However, for me reading has been something I've always been fond of, from spending time at the library with my father and participating in different reading clubs while in elementary school. Reading different books, reading different articles, it's just something that I still enjoy doing regardless.

Amelia: So when you were young, reading seems to have come easy for you?

Monique: Yes, it definitely came easy for me.

Amelia: You were obviously a good reader when you went to college. Did you maintain that or did your appetite for reading change in any way?

Monique: I definitely still had an appetite for reading. However, most of it involved reading for classes as opposed to personal reading at that point. What I noticed in college was even though I was good at reading, that was never a problem, depending upon the subject it became harder for me to retain information. Also at that time, I did not utilize the method of skimming for what I needed. I was more focused on reading everything that was assigned to me by a professor, and oftentimes, as we all know, that can easily be 450 pages per night. So I would find myself struggling to keep up with it and actually mastering and understanding what I was reading.

Amelia: Do you think part of the reason you were having trouble staying engaged with it is because you weren't interested in the topic?

Monique: That definitely played a major part. I struggled mostly with things that related to history. I was just never interested in that topic. So that was always my challenge. However, if it was an English class, that I had no problem with doing, but when it came to anything related to history or science, that's where it became a problem for me.

Amelia: You were probably required to take at least one history and one science. So, how did you end up navigating that reading? Were you using some kind of strategies, were you making notes in the margins or were you underlining what was important or trying to connect what you already knew to the material? How were you doing that?

Monique: What I did was try to take notes and highlight, highlight, highlight and underline what I thought was important, which may not have necessarily been in alignment with what the professor thought was important. That was the strategy I used at the time. If I could go back, I would absolutely use a different strategy and try to connect to different things I was already familiar with to try to remember things.

Amelia: You made some kind of a shift from that college reading experience to where you are now. How did you do that? Did you figure it out on your own?

Monique: I would say I figured it out in graduate school. In graduate school, after taking probably about a semester and a half off, that's when it finally hit me. Also I went for a totally different subject, totally different major. But that's when it hit me that it probably isn't smart to continue to try to read every word, but instead pay more attention to what we discuss in class and then find that part of the reading. And, also try to anticipate where we might go the next day in class. So graduate school is when I finally took the time to say, "There must be a more streamlined way to do the readings that are required of me." But, then again, I also went for something totally different that was much more interesting to me.

Amelia: Say there are college students today who struggle to read but don't discover strategies to overcome that struggle. If they make it through college somehow, could they go into your profession if they're still not proficient readers? Are they going to be able to manage in a position like yours?

Monique: I think they'd be able to function, but I don't think they'd be able to manage as well. It's not just about reading, it's about thoroughly understanding what's being read and being able to take that and apply it to new policies that can be created to make changes federally. If a person can't read, comprehend, and apply it to current-day situations, they would definitely experience some challenges.

Amelia: Is there anything you know about reading now that you wish you had known in college?

Monique: Absolutely. I definitely wish I would have been guided to skim and really look for the major key points to read first, opposed to thinking I had to read all assignments that were given, all pages. If I would have had that strategy as a freshman coming into college, I think I would have done much better.

Amelia: Did you ever have an instructor show you or show the class as a whole how to navigate through a text to find out what's important? Like you said, what a student thinks is important could be way off compared to what an instructor thinks. Did anyone ever show you that? Would it have helped if someone had?

Monique: You know the funny thing is I never had anyone show me that in college or in graduate school. The first time I actually heard somebody say that, honestly, was in January of this year at a training I went to for work, where we were reading through some HUD regulations. That was the very first time I actually heard somebody verbalize that for me.

Amelia: Do you remember what was said?

Monique: Yeah, absolutely. While reading through the guidelines, the instructor gave us homework to read several more pages, and she specifically told us to overlook all of the numbers and everything that was italicized in that section because it was all jargon and mumbo jumbo. She told us to just go past that and it would be much easier to read.

Amelia: Do you wish somebody had told you long ago that it's not always necessary to read everything in a text?

Monique: Absolutely because it did make the reading so much easier.

Amelia: Imagine yourself back in one of your college classes and a faculty member came in, put a book up on a doc cam and said, "I'm just going to take fifteen to twenty minutes before we get started here to show you how I would navigate this chapter, what I'm thinking about as I get through it, and what I'm going to pay attention to." Would you have thought this was too elementary for a college classroom?

Monique: Probably. But if I heard it enough times, I may have stopped to think about it. For example, if I had the opportunity to go into a college classroom and speak to students about a strategy, one thing I might say that they might think I'm totally crazy for is to not read from the first page in a chapter to the end. Actually start at the end where the key highlights are.

Amelia: That's a great point. Knowing how to do that would help a lot of students.

APPENDIX

"The Cough" by Harry Humes

Our young father walked Ash Alley whistling, "Rescue the Perishing," but already he carried mine tunnels home in his black-streaked breath. It was like first sleet against an attic window. My mother would look at him, her lips a line of impatience and fear. "Your lungs will soon be stone," she said. "It's good money, Dorse. It's our only money."

Some of the men who stopped at our house to see my father had tongues like fish that stuck out between words. Gray-faced, shoulders bony, they all seemed about to cave in. My mother would leave the room, her lips thinner than ever, but the cough followed her across the linoleum, down cellar steps, hunkered close when she planted sage and primrose. The cough was like a child. It was always hungry. It demanded attention. It woke us up at odd times and sat in the good chair by the window. In the winter, it trailed behind my father like a peacock feather on a woman's hat.

One summer he told us we were on a planet going nowhere fast. He made a model he called an orrery, and showed us how the heavens worked. The center was bright and hung there like one of my mother's peony blossoms. "That there's what pushes it," he said. "And that's what made the coal."

We looked at him and nodded, but we had our own ideas about what made it go. We could hear it behind the least little thing.

Sources for Content Area Articles and Texts

News Articles
USA Today
U.S. News & World Report
The Washington Post
The Wall Street Journal
The New York Times
The Week
The Tampa Tribune
The Huffington Post
National Post
NY Daily News
The Atlantic
The Seattle Times
The Daily Beast
Forbes

Science
Health & Science
Scientific American
R&D Magazine
Wired
The New York Times
Science Daily

Math
arstechnica.com
The New York Times
Scientific American

More:
Micro Fiction: An Anthology of Really Short Stories
http://www.oprah.com/omagazine/Micro-Fiction-Short-Stories-from-Famous-Writers

Take Ten

Take Ten Minutes to Embed Reading Strategies into Each Class.

- When handing out articles/texts, ask students to write a **prediction** (guess) at the top of the page indicating what the text will be about based on the title. This will access prior knowledge.
- When handing out articles/texts, ask students to write their **purpose** for reading (reason for reading/what they think the author wants them to know) at the top of the page. If students know what they're looking for, their brains will help them find it.
- Ask students to write their **questions** in the margins as they read. At the end of class, use the last ten minutes for students to share their questions aloud. Others might be able to provide the answers. This will encourage students to be aware of their questions, to clarify them, and to search for answers as they read.
- Ask students to write **connections** to the text in the margins as they read. At the end of class, use the last ten minutes for students to share their connections aloud or in writing and discuss how their connections helped them construct meaning within the text.
- Ask students to cross out any unnecessary information as they read. This will create the potential for more focused reading by helping them to **determine what's important** and by keeping extraneous material from muddying the waters as they think through the text.
- Each time you assign a chapter, show your students (using the doc cam and text) what you would pay attention to in the text and what you might **read, scan, or skip.**
- Choose an important paragraph (or even just four or five sentences) to read aloud, and then **jot down** a couple of bullet points of things you find important in the passage and why.

Here's the beauty of it all: Take Ten is a small time investment that yields huge payoffs. You teach your students to be more effective readers with no extra prep and no extra grading. Simply present the task and then place check marks at the tops of students' work as you roam around the room to keep them focused and accountable.

Quick Start to Active Reading

- Select a short, high-interest piece of content-specific text that has abundant opportunities for the application of reading strategies. This can be a short story, a brief article, or an excerpt from a longer piece.
- Before the demonstration, preview the text for potential hot spots where students might be tripped up (for example, figures of speech, historical or political references), then plan some ways to guide them through.
- Anticipate words that might be unfamiliar to students and be prepared to provide strategies to help define them, such as identifying known prefixes, suffixes, roots, context clues, or determining if the word looks or sounds like another word students know.
- Once the demonstration begins, share only the title of the text and provide a prediction, based on the title, of what the text might be about.
- Invite students to provide additional predictions.
- Show students how to determine a purpose for reading by developing questions about the topic, reading any objectives that might have been provided, determining what they want to know or what they suspect the author wants them to know.
- Demonstrate swapping unfamiliar or seldom-used words for words that are more familiar and used in everyday conversation.
- Read aloud, sharing your thinking, jotting down thoughts, questions, visuals, and connections as you move through the text.
- Use text or e-spelling to demonstrate quick annotating.
- While reading, involve students by inviting them to share their thinking.
- When reading is complete, revisit predictions, connections, annotations, definitions, or content.

2

Determining a Purpose

What we see depends mainly on what we're looking for.

—Anonymous

Professional Spotlight

Figure 2.1.

> *Probably one of the most important things in my profession is reading with a goal. If you can read with a goal in mind and keep your mind engaged, you'll pick up on it really fast.*
>
> Jason Brinker, Technical Services Supervisor for an IT/Software company

Chapter 2
Reasonable question: Why are my students having so much trouble focusing while they read? Shouldn't they be beyond that by now?

Imagine you are reading a textbook chapter about the environmental effects of fossil fuels when you encounter the word "car." This triggers a line of thought something like the following: "I have a car. My car is a Honda. It's black. It's old, but I love my car. Hmmm . . . I wonder if I have gas in it. Do I have money to buy gas? I've got a bunch of change in the bottom of my work bag. Where is my bag anyway? Did I leave it in the car? Maybe I left it in the cafeteria this afternoon when I had lunch. I had a grilled cheese for lunch today. Mmmm, my favorite. I'm kind of hungry now."

The entire time these thoughts are running through your mind, you haven't stopped reading. Your eyes are moving through each word, traveling across each sentence in a paragraph, one after another, page after page about the dangers of fossil fuels. In theory, you are still reading. The problem is you're not taking any of it in because you have left the text and are thinking about other things.

Mental triggers, like the word "car," are not the only reason we can be distracted from a text. Often the material is unfamiliar or very difficult to follow. This makes it hard to stay focused. Many times we are simply uninterested in what we are reading. The material is important, we need to know it, but we are bored and are just slogging our way through, struggling to keep our brains engaged.

Our students face these same distractions as they read, and they usually resort to the only remedy they know—rereading. This can be very frustrating ("I didn't have the time to read this the first time, let alone go back and reread it over and over!").

And they are right to be frustrated. Rereading like this is not a very effective way to improve comprehension. Most students will get the same results the second time that they got the first time. Rereading is mainly beneficial when small sections of texts, a sentence or two, need clarification. It generally does not improve overall understanding or retention of the pages and pages of material that make up most academic assignments.

The trick is not in rereading. The trick is in reading once with intentional focus. Students know how prone they are to mentally wandering away from a text. What they don't know is how to cut down on all that wandering by being more focused from the get-go, catching themselves when they do wander, and then refocusing quickly. This is what we need to teach them.

One way to do this is to show students how to determine a purpose before they begin to read. The human brain needs to know what it's looking for in order to find and remember it. We want students to learn from the texts we assign. But if they don't know what they are looking for when they read the material, they won't be able to find it. And if they can't find it, they certainly can't learn it.

Many students don't even know they are supposed to be looking for something when they read. And they are frustrated when they don't find what their instructors think they should. To understand how they feel, imagine you are in a garage filled with random items from ceiling to floor, so packed there is barely room for you to stand. Now imagine that someone calls out, "Did you find it?" What would your response be? Probably something like "Find what? I didn't know I was supposed to be looking for anything!" The key to easing this frustration for students is learning to read with purpose.

There is a simple activity from motivational speaker Tony Robbins that illustrates how important this is. Robbins has his audience look around the room as quickly as possible and mentally note everything they see that is brown. After only a few seconds, he has them stop, focus their eyes to the front, and tell him the brown things they remember. Usually the list is quite long. Next, he tells them to keep their eyes focused squarely ahead and tell him all the things they noticed that were red. The list now is very short. Robbins ends the activity with the prompt, "Seek, and you shall—" To which nearly everyone in the audience responds, "Find."

This is how the human brain works. Give it something to look for, and it will focus on finding it. This same strategy will work for students as they read. If they learn to develop a purpose for reading, it will be much easier for them to stay focused.

GETTING STUDENTS TO BUY IN

The first step in teaching students this strategy is to convince them that it will work. Using the Tony Robbins activity in class is a fun and effective way to do this. You could also show the YouTube video of Robbins demonstrating this to his audience. Another effective YouTube video is titled, "Test Your Awareness: Do the Test." This video is just over a minute long and demonstrates how our brains find and pay attention to exactly what they are looking for. The links to both videos are listed in the Toolbox at the end of this chapter.

As viewers, your students will be told they are taking an awareness test. Then they will be shown a short clip of a basketball game and asked to count how many times the basketball is passed among the players. Most will get the right answer, thirteen. The video will then ask them if they noticed the "moonwalking bear."

The clip will then be replayed, and to students' surprise, they will see that there really is a man in a bear suit gliding across the floor, right through the players. Students will easily see how being given a purpose (counting basketball passes) focused their brains and kept them from being distracted, even by a moonwalking bear.

APPLYING THEIR NEW SKILLS TO READING

Once students see how much more focused their brains are when given a purpose, they will be ready to learn to apply this to reading. A good way to start is with a simple in-class demonstration using a piece of microfiction called "The Diner" by Rhonda Hurst. The full text is included below. Students not only find this activity fun and engaging, but they quickly learn from it how much more effective it is to read when they have a purpose.

"The Diner" by Rhonda Hurst

Third shift at the factory would start in less than an hour. The tiny diner down the street, a local favorite, was packed with workers grabbing a quick bite before clocking in. The diner crew was short-handed as usual. There were only two this time, a young cook and an even younger waitress.

The cook was in the stuffy kitchen working steadily over the hot grill. The back door was propped open, but sweat still poured down his face. He wiped it often with a towel he had over his shoulder. The orders were coming in one after another. He filled the plates and shoved them through the window to the front as fast as he could. He had only dropped one on the floor so far. The burger and tomato had been salvageable. The bun and the fries he had kicked to the side. He'd sweep them up later.

It was noisy out front. People were talking and laughing. Dishes were clinking together. Once in a while, the cook would catch a glimpse of the waitress through the order window. She usually had a tray of food in one hand and somebody's change in the other. Whenever she'd get an empty hand, she'd push her bangs out of her face. The rest of her long hair was pulled back in a loose bun. The cook liked her hair. He told her so every time they worked together. He liked her legs too. "You're gonna run those pretty legs off," he'd say through the window. She'd just laugh and keep moving.

At eleven, the place was empty. The waitress locked the front door and sat down for a minute to catch her breath. She could see her reflection in the broad front windows. One side of her hair was coming loose. She pulled out the bobby pins and shook it all out around her shoulders. Then she got up and started emptying the cash drawer. The diner always did well on the late shift. She stacked the money on the counter as she added it up. Then she put it in the bank pouch next to the register. By midnight, she had cleared away all the food and dishes, wiped everything down, and swept the floor. She took a last look around and spotted a half pitcher of milk under the counter. She had stuck it there when the rush started. It smelled okay, so she carried it to the kitchen. The cook had used up most of the space in the diner's only refrigerator. There was barely enough room for her to squeeze the pitcher in on the bottom shelf. Then she went back out front to turn out the lights and get the money pouch so she could make the night deposit on her way home.

The cook was standing outside the propped open back door smoking a cigarette and waiting for his ride. The waitress turned off the kitchen lights, went outside and locked the door behind her. The night air felt cool on her face. The cook handed her a cigarette and lit it from his. They stood there talking low and smoking in the dark until a car pulled up. The cook got in it with his girlfriend who had come to pick him up, and the two of them drove away. The waitress unlocked her car, threw the money pouch onto the passenger seat, got in and drove out of the empty parking lot.

Begin by giving students copies of the story (either hard copies or e-text) and instructing them to read through it. It is very short and will not take long. Then have students read through the story again, jotting down in the margins everything they think would stand out to a health inspector. Students can do this with a pen on a hard copy or use an annotating feature for e-text.

After a few minutes, have them share their lists with the class and discuss what things they noticed this time that they didn't before. Repeat this process twice more, first from the perspective of a would-be robber and then from the perspective of the cook's girlfriend. Talk briefly about how the changed perspectives gave them a more focused purpose for reading and helped them to zero in on different things in the story.

When students realize that having a purpose helped them more effectively focus on a piece of microfiction, they are better prepared to learn to read their academic texts with purpose. This will require them to do more on their own since they are not going to have an instructor there while they are reading to say "focus on this" or "focus on that." Instead, they need to learn how to develop a purpose by determining on their own what information to look for in a text.

PREREADING STRATEGIES TO DETERMINE PURPOSE

An effective way to help students learn to develop a purpose on their own is to teach them some prereading strategies. One such strategy is to look through a piece of assigned reading for parts that stand out as important, then jot notes in the margins of the text, on a notepad, etc., as reminders of what to look for while reading.

This will require students to do some up-front work, but they can be convinced it will be time well spent if they are reminded of the hours of fruitless rereading they are already doing (not to mention the frustration). Also, the payoff in comprehension, scores on quizzes and tests, and ultimately course grades will make the time spent well worth it.

The first things students should look at are organizational helps (like headings and subheadings) and supplementary material (like chapter objectives and end-of-chapter questions) that have been provided by an author or publisher. For instance, a student might see a heading in a science text that reads "The Process of Osmosis." She can jot down "steps in osmosis process." This will alert her to be looking for specific steps as she reads.

The same thing can be done with chapter objectives and end-of-chapter questions. In a composition textbook, a student might see an objective that says, "Learn to distinguish between uses of formal and informal writing."

He can jot down, "times to use formal writing" and "times to use informal writing." This will focus him to look for these things specifically in the text.

The same student might see the following question at the end of a chapter: "When using information from a source in a research paper, when is it best to directly quote and when is it best to paraphrase?" Jotting down "when best to quote" and "when best to paraphrase" will help him find the answers as he reads.

Students should also know that you, the course instructor, are another source of prereading information. Things you provide (syllabi, study guides, pretests, etc.) typically include specific information that can be used to determine a purpose for reading. Walking students through a few of these will show them how they can make the best use of this type of information.

What an instructor talks about in class can also be used to help develop a purpose. For instance, if you are a history professor, you might assign students to read a chapter on causes of the Civil War. If you focus on three major causes during a class discussion, students will know that these three are especially important and they should look for them as they read.

Also, taking notes on what an instructor covers in class can provide another source for prereading information. The major points that show up in the notes should be points they look for as they are reading assigned texts.

Students who take time for prereading will have a more focused purpose as they read the course material. Their brains will be engaged just like they were when they looked for all the brown things in the room or counted how many times the basketball was passed. And they are less likely to be distracted by trigger words, boredom, or moonwalking bears.

PAUSE AND SUM UP

Another way for students to give their brains a purpose is the "pause and sum up" strategy. This is especially effective if the material is unfamiliar or difficult to understand. Instead of reading straight through long portions of a text, students read one "chunk" at a time, usually just a few paragraphs, a short section with a title or subtitle, etc.

After each chunk, they pause and mentally sum up what they just read. They could even take a moment to jot down the summary in their notes or in the margin of the text. Then they move on to the next chunk and repeat the process. Once they do this a few times, their brains will create a purpose—look for "summarizing" information. Knowing they are going to be summing up helps students focus more quickly on the important points in each chunk of information they read.

MAKING PREDICTIONS

Making predictions is another very effective way to develop a purpose for reading. Predict, in this sense, is just a fancy word for "guess" or "expect." When we're predicting about a text, we're guessing or expecting what we might find in it.

Students are already experts at using this strategy, whether they know it or not. A quick way to show them this is to ask what they do while watching television. "When you're watching the basketball playoffs, do you predict who will make it to the championship game? What about a murder mystery? Do you make predictions about who did it?"

They will quickly realize that they indeed are expert predictors and that this skill keeps them engaged as they watch because they have given their brains a focused purpose—to see if their predictions come true.

The same holds true for reading. Making predictions keeps readers engaged as they seek to determine whether things will be as they expected. Nichols (1983) points out that predicting and speculating helps students develop a purpose for reading, focus on important points in a text, and be more motivated as they read (cited in Fisher and Frey, 2012).

Here again students can use organizational helps and supplementary material provided by an author or publisher to help make predictions. Let's see how an economics instructor we'll call Mara teaches this strategy to her students.

After doing the Tony Robbins activity with her class, she asks, "How did your brains know to look for brown things in the room?"

A few students raise their hands. Mara calls on a young man in the third row back. "You told us to," he says.

"That's right," Mara replies. "And once I said that, looking for brown things became your purpose. When you're reading, who's going to tell you what to look for so you can develop a purpose?"

No one raises a hand now. After a few moments, she lets them off the hook. "Your own ability to make predictions will tell you." Then she spends a few minutes discussing the examples of watching basketball playoffs or murder mysteries on television, encouraging students to share their experiences.

Then Mara explains, "We don't just make predictions out of thin air. We base them on something. For television shows, we mainly base our predictions on things like our own prior experiences, what we know, or what others have told us. When we make predictions about what we are going to read, we need to base them on something too."

Then Mara picks up their class textbook, *Economics for Today* by Irvin B. Tucker. "Let me show you what I mean," she says. The students watch as she flips open to the first page of chapter four. As she does this, she gives them a tip about textbook reading in general. "I don't know about you," she says, "but the first thing I do when I get a reading assignment is to count how many pages are in the chapter. That way I know how long it's going to take me to get through it."

There are a few laughs in the class then. The students get it. Their instructor is talking their language. They've been counting chapter pages since middle school.

Then Mara puts the text up on the doc cam. "In case you're wondering," she adds, "there are twenty-five pages in this chapter including the summary and practice quiz."

At the top of the page showing on the doc cam is the title of the chapter: "Markets in Action." Mara points at it. "This is the chapter title, right?"

The students are watching and nodding.

"Why does the book include this?" she asks.

A student in the front says, "So we'll know what the chapter is about."

"That's right," Mara says. "Titles are something we can use to make our predictions about what we are going to read. The title of this chapter is 'Markets in Action.' I'm going to think about what I know about the words in the title and make a prediction. 'Markets' make me think of shops or businesses. 'Action' makes me think of movement or motion.

So, I could change the words to something more familiar to me and read the title as 'Businesses in Motion.'"

Mara writes "Businesses in Motion" on a sticky note and puts it next to the title (figure 2.2). Then she writes on another sticky note, "I predict this chapter will describe how businesses change, perhaps when they have profits and losses." She puts this up next to the first note.

Then Mara moves down the page and points out a heading. "Authors and publishers give us lots of clues about what's important in a textbook," she says. "Things such as headings like this one, subheadings, summaries, and concepts highlighted in bold help us to focus on the key things to learn, things that are likely to show up on quizzes and tests."

Next, Mara reads the heading aloud: "Changes in Market Equilibrium." Looking at the class, she says, "I know what 'changes' means, and I've already decided that 'markets' might mean businesses. So, what about 'equilibrium'?"

A student offers, "Stability?"

"That's good," Mara replies as she writes "Changes in Business Stability" on another sticky note. Then the class moves on to the subheading, "Changes in Demand," which has a substantial amount of text under it.

Mara asks students to join her this time. "Jot down a prediction for the subheading and feel free to share."

After a few moments, a student seated near the back says, "I think this section is going to talk about how demand for things that are needed or wanted changes. Like for a while people wanted regular TVs, but now people don't want them as much because now they want flat-screen TVs."

"Great prediction," Mara says as she jots "Demand for What People Want or Need Changes" on a sticky note. "Any other predictions?"

A student who has been paying close attention shares that she thinks the section is going to describe what *causes* the demand for items to change. Mara jots "Causes for Change in Demand" on a sticky note and says, "Another great prediction."

The class looks at one more subheading, "Changes in Supply," and repeats the process, developing reasonable predictions together, sharing them aloud, and writing out sticky notes.

Mara tells students that as they read they will have to be on the lookout to see if their predictions are correct and continue to make new predictions as they go along. Then she says, "Now that we've done all of this

Chapter 2

predicting, let's see if we can start to develop a purpose for reading. In other words, what do we want our brains to look for?"

Several students raise their hands. With their input, Mara writes, "We want to find out how the stability of businesses goes up and down because of what customers want and what products are available."

She ends the lesson pleased with the purpose the students have developed and can tell that they are really catching on to how this strategy can help them stay focused as they read.

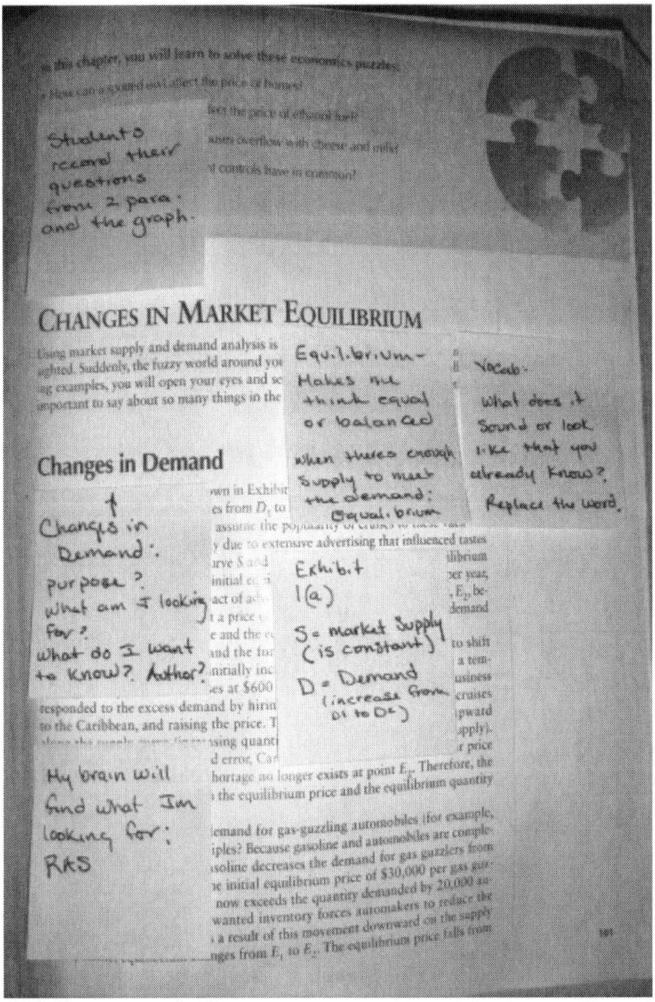

Figure 2.2.

BEING SAVVY READERS

Another way to teach students to read academic material with purpose and focus is to show them that skilled readers do not generally start at the beginning of a chapter in a textbook and read straight through as they would a novel. Nor do they read everything in a chapter. Instead they let their purpose drive which parts they read and the order in which they read them.

Most students have been told to read entire chapters thoroughly. This sounds like a great idea, but it isn't very practical. In fact, it can be self-defeating. Smart readers read only the information that is pertinent to what they need to know. Since teaching students to develop a purpose already involves teaching them to make use of key parts of the text, summaries, end-of-chapter questions, and so on, it is an ideal time to also teach them to be more savvy readers.

For instance, while reading chapter four in that economics textbook, more alert students might skip the sections about "Rigging the Market for Milk" and "Can Vouchers Fix Our Schools?" They might also skip small tidbits of information such as the caption about Adam Smith, who wrote *The Wealth of Nations.* Although this information is interesting and meant to support learning, it is not key for keeping students focused on their developed purpose. They might also read sections in the chapter out of order to more effectively search for answers to their predictions.

MORE HELP TO STAY ENGAGED

Teaching students to develop a purpose is a very effective way to help them beat the "wandering mentally away" problem as they read. But the truth is they are still going to struggle sometimes to stay engaged. This is especially true when students are not interested in the material. Consider this actual comment from a college freshman: "If I am reading something that I'm interested in, I can comprehend that with no problem. It's the things that I don't have very much interest in. I just think it's very boring and I just doze off and think about other things and don't concentrate on the book."

Students are not going to find everything they read in academic texts interesting. They need to learn to stay engaged with the material, boring or not, and to catch themselves when they wander. Below is a list of strategies students can use to be more aware of what they are thinking as they read. Such intentional thinking will help them better recognize when they are drifting away from a text, so they can quickly skim backward and pick up where they left off.

- Try to understand new information by connecting it to something you already know. (If you're reading about how the voting system works in another country, make connections to what you know about how voting works in your country.)
- Visualize characters, settings, concepts, processes, sequences, etc. (If you are reading about a process that has nine steps, picture a train with nine cars sitting on a railroad track. Imagine each car with a picture on the side that helps you remember one of the steps.)
- Ask yourself questions as you read, and then look for the answers. (If you read that John Wilkes Booth killed Abraham Lincoln, ask yourself why he did it, and then look to see if the text tells you why.)
- Mark up a text as you read. (Underline important information, highlight unknown words or unfamiliar phrases, circle important verbs, cross out irrelevant material, restate information in bullet form.)
- Compare or contrast things. (If you are reading about how the human brain works, think about how a brain and a computer are alike or different.)
- Think about how other viewpoints are different from yours. (If you are reading about the death penalty and are against it, think about how you might feel differently if you were in the shoes of someone whose loved one was murdered.)
- Analyze a problem or situation. (If you are reading about a small town that lost nearly half of its businesses and is struggling to recover, think about what caused the problem and try to come up with a solution.)
- Evaluate information. (If you are reading about two studies on the effects of video games on children, one that gives negative results and one that gives positive results, evaluate the quality of the information to decide which one is the most credible.)

The following examples illustrate how an actual student, LaShae, used some of the strategies to keep herself focused, such as asking herself questions, jotting down her thoughts, and underlining (figure 2.3). She also indicates when she caught herself leaving the text, which shows how much more aware she was of her own reading process, even to the point of suspecting her ear infection was affecting her focus (figure 2.4).

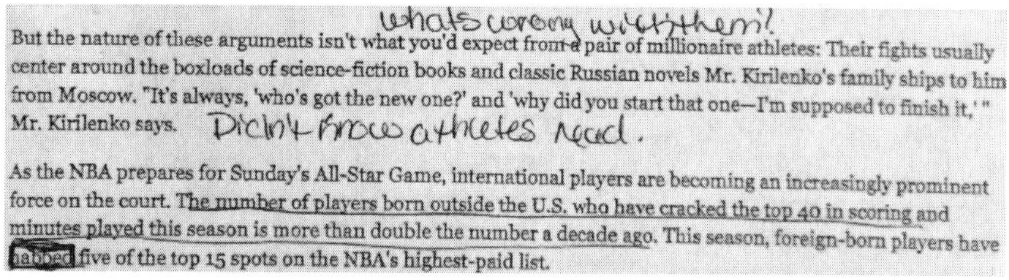

But the nature of these arguments isn't what you'd expect from a pair of millionaire athletes: Their fights usually center around the boxloads of science-fiction books and classic Russian novels Mr. Kirilenko's family ships to him from Moscow. "It's always, 'who's got the new one?' and 'why did you start that one—I'm supposed to finish it,'" Mr. Kirilenko says.

As the NBA prepares for Sunday's All-Star Game, international players are becoming an increasingly prominent force on the court. The number of players born outside the U.S. who have cracked the top 40 in scoring and minutes played this season is more than double the number a decade ago. This season, foreign-born players have nabbed five of the top 15 spots on the NBA's highest-paid list.

[handwritten annotations: "what's wrong with them?", "Didn't know athletes read."]

Figure 2.3.

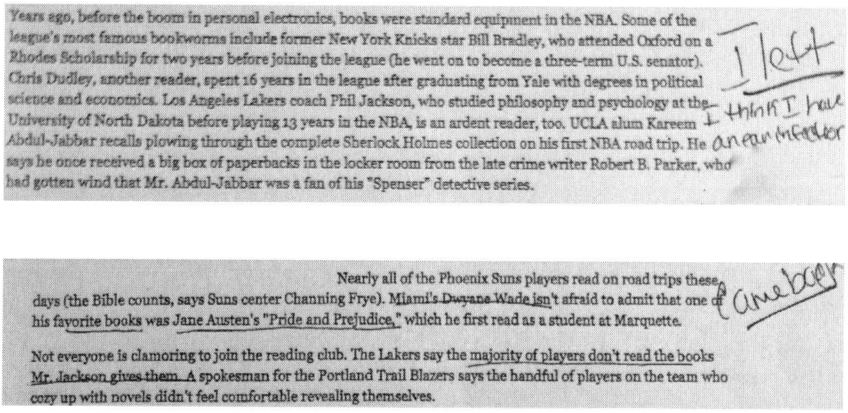

Years ago, before the boom in personal electronics, books were standard equipment in the NBA. Some of the league's most famous bookworms include former New York Knicks star Bill Bradley, who attended Oxford on a Rhodes Scholarship for two years before joining the league (he went on to become a three-term U.S. senator). Chris Dudley, another reader, spent 16 years in the league after graduating from Yale with degrees in political science and economics. Los Angeles Lakers coach Phil Jackson, who studied philosophy and psychology at the University of North Dakota before playing 13 years in the NBA, is an ardent reader, too. UCLA alum Kareem Abdul-Jabbar recalls plowing through the complete Sherlock Holmes collection on his first NBA road trip. He says he once received a big box of paperbacks in the locker room from the late crime writer Robert B. Parker, who had gotten wind that Mr. Abdul-Jabbar was a fan of his "Spenser" detective series.

[handwritten annotations: "I left", "think I have an ear infection"]

Nearly all of the Phoenix Suns players read on road trips these days (the Bible counts, says Suns center Channing Frye). Miami's Dwyane Wade isn't afraid to admit that one of his favorite books was Jane Austen's "Pride and Prejudice," which he first read as a student at Marquette.

Not everyone is clamoring to join the reading club. The Lakers say the majority of players don't read the books Mr. Jackson gives them. A spokesman for the Portland Trail Blazers says the handful of players on the team who cozy up with novels didn't feel comfortable revealing themselves.

[handwritten annotation: "one book"]

Figure 2.4.

THE BOTTOM LINE

As instructors, we spend a lot of time choosing textbooks and determining what we want students to read in those textbooks. Why? Because we care about what we are teaching. And we care about our students. It matters to us that they understand and retain what we want them to learn. That won't happen if students mentally wander away from the text over and over as they try to read. It can be frustrating to us, and it is certainly frustrating to the students. Read what LaShae had to say about that in figure 2.5 below.

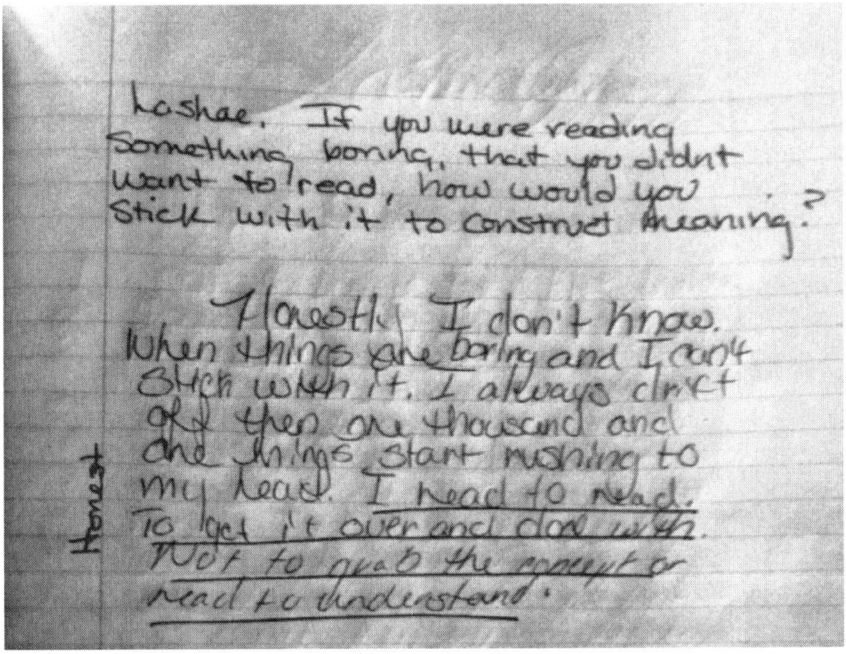

Figure 2.5.

The frustration is hard to miss in her honest comment that she reads "to get it over and done with." How much better if she, and all the other LaShaes in our classrooms, could instead accomplish what she knows is better, to read "to grab the concept or read to understand." Spending time in class to teach the strategies of determining a purpose and making predictions will go a long way toward making this happen.

TOOLBOX

- Facilitate the Tony Robbins activity with students or show Robbins's YouTube video, *How to Have Self Confidence* (http://www.youtube.com/watch?v=tUShaG9ygBM).
- Use the video "Test Your Awareness: Do the Test" to help students see that their purpose will drive their focus (http://www.youtube.com/watch?v=Ahg6qcgoay4).
- Give students this title: "Brain Test May Help Diagnosis: Tool Could Reveal Unseen Damage to Traumatic Injuries," and the list below

of possible purposes for reading the article based on the title. Have students, individually or in groups, evaluate the purposes on a scale of 1 to 5, with 1 being "not specific, not reasonable, not useful" and 5 being "very specific, very reasonable, very useful." Then lead a discussion about their evaluations.

Purposes

1. I want to learn what injuries can be seen from doing this brain test.
2. I am reading this to know what this article is about.
3. How do you get a brain test? What is a brain test?
4. I hope to learn what's revealed in the brain test.
5. Why are they doing the brain test and how is it useful to the person who is getting it done?
6. I hope to learn something new today.
7. To find out what the title is all about.
8. To know how brain testing can actually give you a diagnosis.
9. I hope to learn more about the benefits of brain testing and the advantages it offers.
10. I am curious about the new test.
11. About brain tests and diagnosis.
12. About the different kinds of brain tests.

- The following activity comes from Cris Tovani in her book *I Read It, But I Don't Get It: Comprehension Strategies for Adolescent Readers*. Use Pichert and Anderson's short story, "The House," to demonstrate purpose in the same manner "The Diner" was used in this chapter. After students have read the text, have them read twice more from the perspectives of a real estate agent and a would-be robber.
- Model making predictions with a variety of genres, such as textbooks, newspaper or magazine articles, poems, cartoons, movies, and video clips. For example, show students a cartoon with the caption covered (political cartoons work well). Have them make predictions based on what they see. Then uncover the caption and discuss the accuracy of their predictions.
- Gather a collection of numerous textbook chapter titles, headings, subheadings, chapter objectives, end-of-chapter questions, etc. Have

students use them in class to practice making reasonable predictions and developing relevant purposes for reading. This also works as an effective group activity.

- The following activity for teaching the skill of predicting comes from Harvey Daniels and Nancy Steineke in their book *Text and Lessons for Content-Area Reading.* Lift various sentences from a text. Then give each student an index card that has one of the sentences recorded on it. Allow students a few minutes to come up with a prediction about the text based on their sentence. Then have them move around the classroom, sharing their sentences and predictions aloud with classmates. After students have had an opportunity to share and to listen to several of their classmates' sentences and predictions, have them take their seats and write a more informed prediction about what the text might be about. Then have them read the text on their own and confirm or negate their predictions as they go along and make new predictions if necessary. Remind students that it's not important for predictions to always be correct. It's just important for them to be made. After the reading, discuss how developing predictions gave students something to look for and something to confirm or refute. It also let them know whether they were heading in the right direction and helped them spontaneously make new predictions that were more probable and accurate.

PUTTING IT TO WORK

An effective activity for teaching the importance of determining a purpose involves the story "The Lefft-Ryght Wedding." Begin by asking students to stand shoulder to shoulder in a circle. Then give a student a bag of hard candy and ask him or her to take a piece and hand the bag on until each person has one. Instruct students not to unwrap and eat the candy because they will be using it for the activity.

Next, tell students that you will be reading a short story aloud titled "The Lefft-Ryght Wedding." Each time they hear you say the word "left," they are to hand their piece of candy to the person on their left. When they hear you say the word "right," they are to hand their piece of candy to the person on their right. That is their only job, to listen for the words "left" and "right" and pass their candy accordingly. When they are ready, read the title aloud, "The Lefft-Ryght Wedding," and look around to see if all students have handed their candy first to the classmate on their left and then to the one on their right. When you see all students have done so, confirm that they seem to have the idea and proceed with the story.

Read at a regular pace, paying no attention if the students drop their candy, begin giggling or appear to be struggling to keep up with the pace of the left and right directions. Expect this as students focus their energy mainly on listening for the key words. The text of the story is included below.

"The Lefft-Ryght Wedding" by Rhonda Hurst

The big day finally arrived, the day Lena Lefft would marry Ronald Ryght. For a whole year, Lena Lefft, her mother, Laura Lefft, and her two sisters, Lisa Lefft and Lilly Lefft, had been working hard to make sure everything was just right for the Lefft-Ryght wedding. However, somewhere along the line, every Lefft woman thought she was right and every other Lefft woman was wrong, which left the Lefft family in a state of turmoil, which wasn't right at all.

Rita Ryght, Ronald Ryght's mother, who thought she was right about everything, went to the Lefft house to set things right. When she left, she left the Lefft women right in the middle of a bigger fight than ever. Robert Ryght, Ronald Ryght's father, told his wife, Rita Ryght, that she should have left well enough alone, which left the Ryght family in a big fight too. Larry Lefft, Lena Lefft's father, thought he was right to stay out of the whole thing since his only job was to escort Lena Lefft right down the aisle.

But now the big day was here. The church was full. All the Ryght family guests were on the left side, and all the Lefft family guests were on the right side. Ronald Ryght stood at the front with the preacher on his right and three groomsmen on his left.

Grandma Lefft came in on the right arm of a Lefft family cousin. Grandma Ryght came in on the left arm of a Ryght family cousin. Then came Laura Lefft on the right arm of her son, Lonnie Lefft, followed by Rita Ryght on the left arm of her husband, Robert Ryght. Next came a little Lefft family flower girl tossing rose petals right and left, then three bridesmaids, which rightly included Lisa Lefft and Lilly Lefft.

Finally the "Wedding March" started and all the people stood right up as Lena Lefft came down the aisle with her father, Larry Lefft, escorting her on his left arm, right down to the front where he left her right next to Ronald Ryght. When all the right words were said, Ronald Ryght kissed his bride, Lena Lefft-Ryght, and the happy couple turned right around and faced the congregation. The preacher said, "May I introduce you to Mr. and Mrs. Ronald Ryght." Everyone forgot about being angry and left filled with joy. So the Lefft-Ryght wedding turned out right after all.

When the story ends, ask who has the most candy and who doesn't have any candy at all. At this point, students are usually laughing at their own inability to keep up with the simple instructions and the physical demands of passing their candy.

Next, ask students to take their seats and tell them they are to write a three-or-four-sentence summary of the story that they will share aloud. The expressions on their faces will reveal their concern. They won't be expecting to have to recall the story.

After a couple moments, rescue students by telling them they don't really have to write the summary. Then lead a discussion about why the task would have been challenging and how that relates to reading with a purpose. Make sure the following points come out:

- Students had trouble remembering what the story was about because they were not focused on the story line. They were focused on listening for the words and passing the candy. That was their purpose, and that was the thing on which their brains chose to concentrate. The human brain will find and pay attention to exactly what it's looking for.
- It's the same with reading. Our brains will focus on our purpose, our reason for reading, what we want to know or what the author wants us to know.
- If we're reading without a purpose, we won't find the information we need to remember. Our eyes will travel through sentences like a loose wheel rolling down the street with no idea where it's going.

This activity could be followed up by showing the YouTube video mentioned earlier, "Test Your Awareness: Do the Test," (http://www.youtube.com/watch?v=Ahg6qcgoay4).

PROFESSIONAL SPOTLIGHT READING INTERVIEW
WITH JASON BRINKER

Title: Technical Services Supervisor for an IT/Software company
Location: College Station, Texas

Amelia: What type of reading is required the most in your profession?

Jason: In my job, there is a lot of technical documentation required. We need to read manuals for a myriad of different IT products as well as different protocols for our business IT service.

Amelia: When you're doing this technical reading, what is the length? Are you talking about small chunks, pages and pages, or chapters and chapters?

Jason: If I know specifically what I'm looking for, I can typically jump right to it in the technical manual for the equipment I use. However, if I don't know exactly what we're looking to do or the capabilities of the equipment they want to use, it could be ten to fifteen pages, but not past fifteen.

Amelia: You said, if it's something you're familiar with you can kind of skip and jump in where you need to. How do you determine what's important enough to look at and what isn't?

Jason: It's my experience. When I'm dealing with equipment and I'm reading through a technical manual, they want to tell me about why the feature is in there and how it can save me money, things like that. I don't care. I really just need to know about the feature. I basically weed out the sales pitch.

Amelia: How do you do that? Do you skim through the reading, see things like that, and then skip them?

Jason: Yeah, I just skim things usually.

Amelia: And then you just move on?

Jason: Yep.

Amelia: How do you go about thinking through the vital information to understand what you are reading?

Jason: In a typical situation, I'm given a task. That task could be to find a product to research to determine if it fits into our business needs. I know how our software is delivered to the end user, and I use that knowledge to look through the capabilities of the equipment I'm researching to be sure the product will work. I make sure it supports the multiple protocols or fulfills a particular function, and then I read through the documentation to determine ease of use. In an IT business, the little details need to be taken into account on all products, and I always reread to make sure I didn't miss something that could affect my end purpose.

Amelia: If there are students coming out of college with degrees, but they aren't proficient readers, could they still qualify for a job working with you? If so, how would they get around the reading deficit?

Jason: That's more of a management question in terms of if they will be hired if they're not proficient in technical reading. I won't necessarily have that expectation when they first get hired on, but it will be something I expect them to learn by experience. I will see to that personally. I will tell them to go find this particular feature in the manual, and I'll make them do that. When I tell my guys to go find something, they know I don't like them to just regurgitate information. I don't want a definition. I want an *operational* definition. I want them to understand how it works. That can only come from doing the research and reading through the manual. So, there are two things my guys know. They'll put them on my gravestone. "Get better, faster" and "Give me an *operational* definition, don't just give me a definition."

Amelia: Let's say someone gets hired and you give them some opportunities to go find operational definitions and they can't do it. Would you find ways to remediate or would you dismiss them?

Jason: That's a tough question because I like to believe everybody can learn, and I've yet to find anybody I couldn't teach. But quite honestly, I wouldn't have much use for them if they couldn't do it. It's so important. I would expect it to be a daily function of their job. They would have to learn how to do it. If they couldn't, I'd look to see if there was another position somewhere else and move them out.

Amelia: It sounds like it would be labor intensive to teach someone when you probably have a host of other candidates who are more able to do that.

Jason: Yeah. It would be great if I took a guy who came right out of school, for instance, and he could do exactly what I told him if I said, "Use this wire. Look at this protocol. I want you to tell me how it works." I'd want him to come back and give me everything I was looking for, and say, "It works like this. This piece of equipment works. Here's an alternative from the same vendor. We can use this." That's a huge part of training that I wouldn't have to do. I would definitely consider him over somebody who couldn't do that. Unfortunately I don't get to give them a technical reading test before they get hired at my company.

Amelia: How are people generally hired?

Jason: Most of the people who work for me have been promoted into the position. I don't hire them off the street. Not that we wouldn't. It's just that we haven't found any candidates we could. They'd have to start somewhere else in the company, get some experience, and then be moved into that position.

Amelia: If students are coming to you straight out of school, where would they start?

Jason: Some have started in phone support. Somebody calls in and says, "I need to do this, my printer doesn't work, or my router doesn't work." It's in that position someone hired in would start learning technical reading skills. We write our own manuals. So, they're reading these manuals while assisting someone over the phone. I've got two people who started out like that. Right off the bat, they're learning technical reading.

Amelia: Are there tests for people hired in those jobs?

Jason: We have another company that tests first. They run a whole testing scope where they test technical knowledge, comprehension, how quick someone is to learn. I don't think it has a technical reading side of it. It doesn't especially test for that.

Amelia: When you hired in, how did you learn technical reading? Did you have these skills from school? How did you get to the point where you are now?

Jason: I have the ability to remember about 90 percent of what I read. It's kind of one of those things that comes naturally to me, but I do want to say I learned quite a bit more on the job than in school. There have been some times it was kind of rough. I was trying to figure out what I was reading. Trying to figure out something in a technical manual is boring. I would always get distracted. Now I can go through that tech manual, find where I need to be, find what I'm looking for and have the answer.

Amelia: Is it because you're now familiar with it? If you switched jobs, would you struggle again?

Jason: No. I've learned how to do it now. Also, we look at so many pieces of standard equipment. If I switch companies and they ask me to look at something, there's a very good possibility I will already know how it works or be able to quickly figure it out.

Amelia: Is there anything you wish you'd known before you got the job that you think college students should know?

Jason: I think probably the biggest thing is if they're going into an IT company, that's what their degree is in, they need to learn to read technical manuals and comprehend them quickly. The number one thing that would be helpful is some kind of way to stay on task. It is boring to read through tech manuals, and your mind starts to wander unless you're super interested in it or if you have a specific goal to look for something. I mean that was my only thing, it's just boring. You need some kind of exercise when you're reading to keep your mind on task.

Amelia: So your mind wanders if it's boring and you don't have a specific purpose for reading?

Jason: Yeah. If I'm looking for a certain protocol that works with a specific router, that always helps me stay focused, or if I'm looking for a specific item or I'm trying to learn how to do something and I need to learn how to do it. Probably one of the most important things in my profession is reading with a goal. If you can read with a goal in mind and keep your mind engaged, you'll pick up on it really fast. I talk to my guys and their biggest complaint is they read something three times because they keep getting distracted.

APPENDIX

"The House" by J. W. Pichert and R. C. Anderson

The two boys ran until they came to the driveway. "See, I told you today was good for skipping school," said Mark. "Mom is never home on Thursday," he added. Tall hedges hid the house from the road, so the pair strolled across the finely landscaped yard. "I never knew your place was so big," said Pete. "Yeah, but it's nicer now than it used to be since Dad had the new stone siding put on and added the fireplace."

There were front and back doors and a side door that led to the garage, which was empty except for three parked 10-speed bikes. They went in the side door, Mark explaining that it was always open in case his younger sisters got home earlier than their mother.

Pete wanted to see the house, so Mark started with the living room. It, like the rest of the downstairs, was newly painted. Mark turned on the stereo, the noise of which worried Pete. "Don't worry, the nearest house is a quarter mile away," Mark shouted. Pete felt more comfortable observing that no houses could be seen in any direction beyond the huge yard.

The dining room, with all the china, silver, and cut glass, was no place to play so the boys moved into the kitchen where they made sandwiches. Mark said they wouldn't go to the basement because it had been damp and musty ever since the new plumbing had been installed.

"This is where my dad keeps his famous paintings and his coin collection," Mark said as they peered into the den. Mark bragged that he could get spending money whenever he needed it since he'd discovered that his dad kept a lot in the desk drawer.

There were three upstairs bedrooms. Mark showed Pete his mother's closet that was filled with furs and the locked box that held her jewels. His sisters' room was uninteresting except for the color TV that Mark carried to his room. Mark bragged that the bathroom in the hall was his since one had been added to his sisters' room for their use. The big highlight in his room, though, was a leak in the ceiling where the old roof had finally rotted.

3

Determining What's Important

Readers of nonfiction have to decide and remember what is important in the texts they read if they are going to learn anything from them.

—Harvey & Goudvis

Professional Spotlight

Figure 3.1.

When I started to figure out the strategies, I said, "This is not so bad." I realized I didn't need to read every single word. I learned that in graduate school. You don't have to read every single word. Then you develop strategies for how to whittle down the information into bite size-pieces.

Shenita Brokenburr, PhD, Vice President of a Non-Profit Organization

Chapter 3
Reasonable question: My students think *everything* in the text is important. How can I teach them to be discriminating readers?

Imagine a college student facing his first reading assignment in a political science class: "Read chapter one by Friday." He sits down, accesses his e-textbook, and discovers, to his dismay, that chapter one is fifty-nine pages long, has fourteen headings, thirty-one subheadings, twenty-four charts and graphs, and over a dozen sidebars. With no real sense of direction, he begins to slog his way through like a tourist lost in the Amazon. It doesn't take long before he is mired in what seems like an endless bog of details with no idea how he got there or where to go next.

The problems faced by this reader are not rare. According to the University of Alabama, reading is required in 85 percent of college work. Students on campus after campus, semester after semester, struggle to navigate their way through the pages and pages of assigned text.

A main reason this challenge is so difficult is that many college readers are unable to discriminate between what is important in academic material and what is supporting or even irrelevant detail. They do not know how to focus on what they need to learn from a text, nor do they know how to let that focus guide their reading decisions. Instead, they sit down and blindly try to read everything assigned from beginning to end, wrongly assuming that it all must be of equal importance.

This has two common results, both negative. The first is wasted time. Some students will read hour after hour, wasting time on minor details that could have been used on major concepts. This is counterproductive not only for students but for instructors as well. We want the students in our classes to learn the content material in the most effective ways possible. Wasted time is not effective.

The second common result is ditched reading assignments. Some students get so frustrated that they give up reading altogether, hoping instead to get everything they need from in-class sources, such as lectures and instructor-created visual presentations. Since there is no guarantee that everything that is important to learn will be directly covered in class, students can easily find themselves falling behind and unprepared for tests, presentations, and other coursework. Giving up on reading assigned texts also robs students of the opportunity of becoming more adept at engaging and learning academic material on their own.

FOCUSED READING ASSIGNMENTS

There are several things that can be done to help students become more discriminating readers. One is to be more discriminating ourselves in what we assign.

Most college reading assignments are of the "Read chapter one by Friday" variety, which offer students no specific directions to help them focus their time and energy. Couple this with the promise of a quiz to hold students accountable and you have a sure recipe for hours of frustrating reading.

Consider how the following assignment is different:

In your Medical Law and Ethics *text, read chapter three and make connections to what was previously discussed in class about the legal system as it relates to health care. Be prepared to share your insights by Monday online in our class forum.*

Below are particular areas of focus:

- *Medical Practice Acts, pp. 57–58*
- *Licensure of the Physician, pp. 58–61*
- *Statute of Limitations, p. 63*

A student with this type of assignment can quickly determine a clear focus for reading and more effectively zero in on what is important and what isn't.

INTENTIONAL FOCUS

Another way to help students learn to be more discriminating readers is to directly teach the skills they need to be able to independently identify the most important parts in a text and to motivate themselves to be invested *in* and focused *on* those parts.

One of the first things they need to know is that they are *supposed* to be intentionally invested and focused as they read academic material. In order to take in, remember, and use information, there has to be a level of deliberate effort. It might seem obvious, but the truth is most students have not considered the idea that they should purposefully engage with targeted information. Reading without intentional focus is like listening without intentional focus—information goes in one ear, across the brain with limited engagement, then out the other ear.

You can illustrate this with a simple example. Ask students to imagine they are sitting alone in a crowded fast-food restaurant. There are conversations going on all around them, but they are busy eating and not really paying attention. Then say, "You are hearing everything said, but how much of it will you remember five minutes after you leave?" Students will quickly realize the answer is "not much."

Now ask them to imagine themselves in that same restaurant and they hear a person in the next booth begin telling a juicy story about someone they know. Now how much will they remember five minutes after they leave? It is easy for students to recognize that more personal investment leads to more deliberate effort to focus attention.

Once students realize they have this strong natural ability to intentionally focus, they are ready to learn strategies to help them apply it to reading.

READ, SCAN, OR SKIP?

One such skill is deciding what to read, what to scan, and what to skip based on one's purposes for reading. Telling students they don't have to read every word and sentence in academic texts will certainly capture their attention. This is often in direct conflict with what they have been taught during their K–12 education. Students are educationally raised to believe good readers don't "skip" parts of the texts. If a teacher tells them to read chapter five, students might even view such skipping as "cheating."

It will be a major relief for students to realize that skilled readers of academic material do not read everything with the same level of attention. Instead they make reading decisions based on their purposes for reading. If your students do not know what it means to read with specific purposes in mind or how to develop such purposes, there are strategies in chapter two, "Determining a Purpose," that can be used to teach this skill.

There are some basic things students will need to keep in mind. First, most college-level reading is multilayered. As a result, students will find themselves having multiple purposes for reading. For instance, some of the more general purposes are to learn facts and concepts, to build on previously learned material, and to analyze or evaluate new material. Another common purpose for reading is to focus on information needed to accomplish a task, such as study for a test, participate in a discussion, post in a forum, or write a paper.

Once students have determined their purposes for reading, they can learn to use those purposes to decide what to read, scan, or skip.

One of the first things a skilled reader with purposes in mind should do is to scan the assigned text to make initial decisions about what should be given the most priority. There are common elements in academic texts, such as headings, subheadings, sidebars, summaries, charts, and graphs students can use to make reading decisions.

For example, imagine a student is reading a chapter in a sociology text about the rapid change in American business in the twentieth century, and one of his purposes is to identify the impact this had on gender roles. If he is scanning the text and sees the following heading "World War II, Women, and the Workforce," he can quickly mark that as an important section to read. If he sees a subheading that says "Politics of the Board-room," he might mark it as something to scan. A sidebar titled "The Model T Put Business on the Road" could be something to skip.

Once students have marked sections in a text, they can decide how to order them for reading. For instance, the student with the sociology text might start by scanning the "Politics of the Boardroom" subheading to see if it contains information about gender roles. If so, he can re-mark it as a "read" section. If not, he can skip it. Also, suppose he marked a section to read titled "Stay-at-Home Fathers." Even though that one comes after the "World War II, Women, and the Workforce" section, he might read it first because his instructor just talked about stay-at-home fathers in class and it is fresh in the student's mind.

Students are often resistant to doing any kind of prereading like this because they think it will take a lot of extra time. However, once they try it and see how much time they can actually save, their resistance quickly fades.

ANNOTATING A TEXT

Another important skill students need to learn is to annotate as they read. Students tend to resist this strategy as well and for the same reason. Many think to themselves, "I don't like reading. Why would I drag out the process even longer?"

It's true that marking up a text (either with a pen or annotation features on an e-device) will take more time initially, but it will save time later by cutting down on the need to reread. Also reviewing for quizzes and tests can be much easier and faster using an annotated text.

Another thing students might resist is actually writing on a text instead of just using a highlighter. Highlighters don't make notations about important sections, don't record thoughts or questions, don't jot key points, don't engage readers. A college student said it best when she told a fellow classmate, "That highlighter isn't going to do the thinkin' for you."

Instructors can illustrate this with a simple demonstration. Display a copy of a textbook page that has been heavily highlighted in front of the class and ask students to look at it and decide what the reader was thinking about the highlighted sections (figure 3.2).

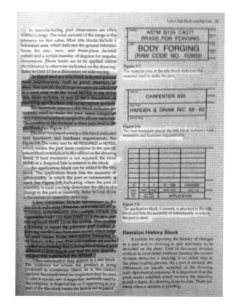

Figure 3.2.

Students might be able to say the reader seemed interested in the page because it was highlighted a lot or that the reader must have thought nearly all of it was important, maybe for different reasons because of the use of different colors.

Then ask how well it appears the reader could use the highlighted page to prepare for a quiz or a test. Even with the use of different colors, the reader will still need to do quite a bit of rereading to recall important points in the text.

Next, show students a sample of an annotated page (figure 3.3). Discuss how this more effectively shows the reader's thinking and provides focused study notes that can prevent a lot of unnecessary rereading. End with a short discussion about how much more engaged with a text a reader can be by annotating instead of highlighting and how such engagement can enhance learning and make reading time more productive.

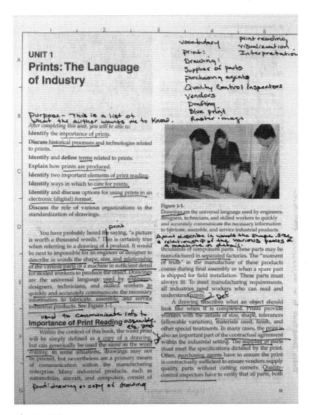

Figure 3.3.

INTENTIONAL READING DEMONSTRATION

The most effective way to teach students to be more discriminating readers is to do a classroom demonstration that illustrates how to read with intentional focus. During such a think-aloud, students will be able to more clearly understand how to decide what to read, what to scan, and what to skip. They can also be shown strategies for making meaningful notations and creating connections between known and unknown information.

Below is an example of this type of demonstration using an article titled "Four Parenting Styles and How They Influence Child Behavior" by author and educator Kendra Cherry. The full text of the article is in the appendix at the end of this chapter.

Display the article in front of the class. Be sure to use a format that allows you to mark the text, by hand or electronically, while the students watch.

Read the title aloud. Then jot down a purpose for reading in the margin: To identify the four styles of parenting and to understand how they influence child behavior.

Tell students you are going to start by scanning the whole article to decide what to read, what to scan, and what to skip. Begin by pointing out that the first two paragraphs seem to be mainly background on the overall topic. Mark those "skip."

Next quickly look over paragraph three with students. From the first sentence, it seems this part will be about things that shape parenting styles. Though this doesn't appear to be directly focused on your identified purpose for reading, the paragraph contains a bulleted list and key words in bold that might provide useful information. Mark that paragraph "scan."

Point out that paragraph four seems to contain more background information. Mark it "skip."

Then move on to the first heading, "The Characteristics and Effects of Parenting Styles." Point out the subheadings that list the four parenting styles in bold. Say to students, "This section is directly related to my purpose." Then mark the section "read."

Now go to the next heading, "How Do Parenting Styles Form?" Say, "This one seems interesting but is not directly related to my purpose."

Mark it "skip." Do the same with the last heading, "The Limitations of Parenting Styles."

Now talk briefly about what you are going to read first. "I think I will start with the information I marked 'read' because it is directly related to my purpose. Then I will go back and scan through paragraph three to see if there is anything else useful there."

Explain that as you read you are going to do three other things that will help you intentionally focus your reading—determine what material is needed and strike out what isn't needed, make notations of important points, and create connections between known and unknown information to help you remember those points. Take a few moments to explain why these three strategies are effective.

Determining what is needed and striking out what isn't requires differentiating between three types of information readers will encounter:

- Information that is important and relates to the purpose for reading
- Information that is interesting but doesn't relate to the purpose for reading
- Information that is neither important nor interesting and doesn't relate to the purpose for reading

Students generally have little difficulty with the first and third types of information because the relevance or lack of relevance to the purpose is easy to determine. However, they have more trouble with the second type. When they encounter interesting information, their attention is drawn to it, and they have a more difficult time determining what they should strike out.

Instructors can help here by explaining that striking out information doesn't mean it is not important. It just means that it is not relevant to a reader's focused purpose. If it's not relevant, it's not needed. Getting unneeded material out of the way makes it easier to focus on what's left.

Another strategy is to concentrate on looking for key points in a text, then briefly summarizing them in the margins, on a sticky note, or an electronic notepad. This is useful for two reasons. First, summarizing information in our own words helps us think through that information. Second, notations serve as visual reminders of important material and provide a quick reference for review.

A third way for students to focus on important material is to connect it to things they already know. Creating connections helps readers more easily understand new information. It also works as a mental cue to help them remember important facts and concepts.

To demonstrate these three things, read aloud the first point in the section marked "read," quickly striking out unneeded words and phrases as you go (see example below). Tell students that though some of the material is interesting, it is not directly related to your purpose.

> **Authoritative Parenting:** ~~Authoritative parents have~~ clear rules and guidelines ~~for their kids, but they are also~~ responsive and willing to explain the reasoning behind the rules. ~~They~~ listen to their kids, ~~but are~~ not punitive or rejecting when their children make mistakes. ~~Baumrind suggested that these parents are~~ supportive and monitor their children's behavior ~~carefully in order to~~ offer boundaries and feedback ~~without being intrusive or restrictive.~~
>
> ~~Experts tend to agree that authoritative parenting is the overall best approach that~~ produces children who are capable, happy, self-confident, and successful.

After you have finished striking out unneeded material under the first point, go back and look at what is left. From this, articulate a quick list of characteristics of authoritative parenting and jot it in the margin:

Authoritative Parenting

- Clear rules and guidelines, reasoning explained
- Parents listen and don't punish or reject when children make mistakes
- Parents supportive and monitor their children's behavior
- Parents offer boundaries and feedback
- Children capable, happy, self-confident, and successful

Next, pause to consider a possible connection to the material. For instance, you might say, "I've seen this in action. My Aunt Theresa used this style of parenting with her children." Jot down "Aunt Theresa" near your list.

Move through the remaining three parenting styles one at a time, striking out unneeded information, jotting down notations, and drawing on background knowledge to make connections.

After this, go back and scan through paragraph three, noting any useful information found there.

Wrap up the demonstration by quickly taking students back through your notations to show them how they helped you stay focused on fulfilling your purpose of identifying the four styles of parenting and understanding how they influence the behavior of children. Point out how students can use the notes to review for quizzes or tests.

Instructors sometimes question whether demonstrations like this are any more effective at helping students learn reading strategies than a more straightforward approach of simply telling the students what they need to do. The old adage "a picture is worth a thousand words" applies here. Students will learn much more from what they see us do than from what they hear us say.

Research has shown over and over that modeling is one of the most effective teaching strategies. While it is true that this often takes more time and effort on our part, it is also true that it pays off in big dividends for our students.

THE BOTTOM LINE

Academic texts play a vital (and hefty) role in the college educational process. Students need to effectively navigate their way through all of that reading to effectively learn from all of that reading. The reality is that many students aren't effectively navigating. They have never learned to be discriminating readers, so they waste hours and hours slogging through every detail or they give up out of frustration and ditch reading altogether, neither of which results in effective learning.

By taking the time to teach students the skills they need, we will not only be helping them know how to navigate their way through fifty-nine pages, fourteen headings, thirty-one subheadings, twenty-four charts and graphs, and over a dozen sidebars. We will be helping them know how to *learn* from all those pages, headings, subheadings, charts, graphs, and sidebars.

TOOLBOX

- Give students a copy of a two- to three-page article and provide them with a specific purpose for reading it. Then have them work through the article, striking out unneeded material, jotting notations, and making personal connections in the same fashion as the reading demonstration described in this chapter.
- After initial instruction and an overall demonstration of discriminating reading strategies, conduct mini-demonstrations once a week for three or four weeks. These can be done during the first five minutes of class, using different sections of content-area texts to quickly model one specific strategy each week. This will solidify learning and also model how to use the strategies on the specific types of reading material students will encounter in your class.
- Ask student volunteers to place their text on the doc cam and share their reading decisions about what to read, scan, or skip.
- Have students work on their own to label sections of an assigned text with either "read, scan, or skip." A two- to three-page section from the course textbook or a short content-related article works well for this activity. Have students come together in groups of three or four to compare their reading decisions and the rationale behind them.
- Have students read a brief article or a couple of pages from a textbook chapter using a pen to note points they think are important. When they are finished, have them jot down a list of the ten most important points. Then pair students up and have them share their responses and then create another list of what the two of them together think are the ten most important points. Then put two pairs together and have the four students discuss their lists and give a rationale for the points they included. This will help students begin to be more intentional about deciding what is important in a text and will let them see how other students make these decisions.
- After lessons on reading strategies, use one or more of the following prompts to help students consider what they understand about the strategies and what more they need to know. Write the prompt on the board, then give students five minutes to respond in writing. These can be done just to let students reflect or can be handed in to let you know what they are thinking.

This is what caught my attention:
This is what I discovered today:
This is an example of how I can use this reading strategy:
This will work for me! Here's how I am going to use it:
This is what I know about determining what's important when reading:
This is how I determine what I can scan and what I can skip:
Here's what makes finding what's important difficult for me:
Here's what makes reading a textbook difficult for me:
These are the changes I need to make to improve my reading:
This is what went well and what I could have done better:
This is what's helping me learn:
Here's how things are going:
Here's how I'm changing as a reader:
Today in class I learned . . .
I really need to know more about . . .
I'd like the instructor to know . . .

- Have students make a chart like the one below. Give them a copy of a two- to three-page article along with a specific purpose for reading it. Then have them read the article and mark the following: what is interesting but not relevant to their purpose, what is important and relevant to their purpose. Then have them jot a list under each heading in the chart. This exercise helps students learn to differentiate between types of information by not only having them focus as they read, but by also articulating their findings in words.

Interesting but not relevant	Important and relevant

Figure 3.4.

PUTTING IT TO WORK

The article below can be used in any class to demonstrate the value of striking out unneeded material to be able to focus more effectively on the main points of a text.

Use the title, "Factors Leading to Increased Recidivism Rates of Mentally Ill Parolees," to help students come up with a purpose for reading. You might start with something like the following: What does the term "recidivism" mean?" From there, lead students in a short discussion to help them isolate a focus question: What factors have led to increased recidivism rates of mentally ill parolees?

Then lead students through the article, demonstrating how to strike out material that does not directly pertain to the purpose. For instance, in the introduction, you might strike out everything except "Shifts in public policy, a lack of mental health services, and inadequate parole supervision are serious contributing factors to the high recidivism rates."

In the "Shifts in Public Policy" section, you might strike out the first and last sentences, leaving only the two in the middle that describe the shift to deinstitutionalize the mentally ill.

You can choose to continue through the rest of the article as a class, do just the first few sections and let students practice with the rest on their own, or let them work in groups.

Once all unneeded material is crossed out, show students how to go back and read through what is left to find the answer to their focus question.

End by discussing how this strategy can help them more effectively focus on the "meat and potatoes," the parts of a text that are important for their reading purpose.

"Factors Leading to Increased Recidivism Rates of Mentally Ill Parolees" by Kiernan Gamel

Introduction

A major mental health policy issue is the recidivism rate of mentally ill parolees. Shifts in public policy, a lack of mental health services, and inadequate parole supervision are serious contributing factors to the high recidivism rates among this underserved segment of the mentally ill population. As a result, growing numbers of offenders with mental illness are repeatedly cycling through correctional systems across the country.

Shifts in Public Policy

Shifts in public policy have had a major impact on the recidivism rates of individuals suffering from mental illness. One such policy shift involved de-institutionalizing the mentally ill. This resulted in individuals who suffered from mental illness being systematically moved out of state public mental hospitals. From 1955 to 1980, the resident population in those facilities fell from half a million to just over 150,000.

In the 1990s, institutions began to close in significant numbers. Many leaders in the psychiatric community argued that moving patients out of state hospitals and into community-based outpatient settings represented a humane alternative to overcrowded and understaffed institutions. Unfortunately, in most cases the closing of state hospitals was not accompanied by the promised number of clinics and halfway houses necessary to care for released hospital patients. One result was a rise in the number of those with mental illness becoming involved with the criminal justice system and eventually prison.

Another public policy shift that had a major impact on the mentally ill was the anti-drug campaign during the Nixon and Reagan years. This campaign, popularly known as the "war on drugs," drew on Nancy Reagan's coined phrase "just say no" and set the stage for zero tolerance policies concerning drug use. These zero tolerance laws surrounding drug use made those with mental illness especially vulnerable to involvement with the criminal justice system due to the high prevalence of substance misuse among the mentally ill, especially those with schizophrenia or bipolar disorders. This shift in policy also led to greater numbers of the mentally ill entering the prison system.

Lack of Mental Health Services

While in prison, many mentally ill inmates do not receive any mental health care. If they do receive treatment, it typically consists of a very brief psychiatric evaluation and a medication regimen. Ongoing therapy is seldom offered. When it is offered, such treatment is often ineffective because mentally ill inmates tend to distrust mental health workers who are employed by prison systems.

When inmates with mental illness are paroled, they often face difficult challenges that put them at risk for failure. One of these is limited access to medication. Often those who suffer from mental illness and have been on psychotropic medication are released from prison with a 30-day supply of these meds and have no means to obtain refills. When the medication is gone, the parolees soon begin another cycle of emotional and mental insta-bility, leading to parole violations and return to prison.

Not only do they lack the ability to obtain medication, they do not have easy access to other mental health care. In many cases, the main criterion used to decide who qualifies for mental health services is the degree to which a person is considered an imminent danger to self or others. Many parolees showing up for services at mental health clinics do not meet this criterion. As a result, they are seldom seen. Instead, they are referred to local medical clinics that have no specialization in treating mental health disorders and lack the government funding needed to supply such treatment.

Even if such services were available, parolees often cannot access them because of a lack of transportation. Many do not have a valid driver's license and do not have money for public transportation or even to purchase a bicycle. This not only prevents them from getting mental health care, but also makes it very difficult for them to participate in other social supports such as Alcoholics Anonymous or Narcotics Anonymous.

Inadequate Parole Supervision

Another factor that affects overall recidivism rates for the mentally ill is the role played by parole agents. They are a major part of the system designed to assist former inmates. However, parole agents are not always equipped to help those with mental illness. Two reasons for this are their enormous case-loads and the fact that they are not specifically trained to deal with the problems faced by the mentally ill. Consequently many parolees with mental illness are not monitored effectively, which adds to the likelihood that they will discontinue their medication (if they have any to begin with) and begin to experience symptoms of their disorders.

Also, as the size of the overall parole population has grown, the ways in which parole agents manage their case loads has gone from a traditional re-entry facilitator approach to a more surveillance oriented and punitive approach. Parole agents are also more likely to have a law enforcement background and embrace a control model of parole supervision that focuses more on surveillance and detection and less on treatment and rehabilitation.

Conclusion

Shifts in public policy, a lack of mental health services, and inadequate parole supervision have created a devastating cycle for many with mental illness. Those who have no safety net, such as family to care for them, find it very difficult to effectively integrate into society. As a result, they end up on a merry-go-round of crisis interventions, hospitalizations, homelessness, and repeated incarceration. This is a major issue in mental health policy that must be addressed to prevent the endless recycling of the mentally ill through America's correctional systems.

PROFESSIONAL SPOTLIGHT READING INTERVIEW WITH SHENITA BROKENBURR, PHD

Title: Vice President of a Nonprofit Organization
Location: Chicago, Illinois

Amelia: Can you describe the kind of reading required in your profession?

Shenita: Peer-reviewed publications on specific subject matter dealing with talent management, human resources, anything dealing with hiring, retiring, firing, or inspiring people. I read a lot of online publications as well. I read a lot of policy briefs from the Society for Human Resource Management.

Amelia: When you're reading this type of material, are you doing it because you want to be better, a master of your craft type thing, or are you reading it because you're required to?

Shenita: I am a person who wants to be the very best I can be at my craft and in my profession. So, I am very passionate about the work that I do. It is a requirement, but more than that I enjoy reading it and I enjoy learning, and reading is fundamental to that.

Amelia: I heard you say something a moment ago about doing online reading. What percent of your reading is online compared to hardcopy?

Shenita: I would say probably 60/40 with online being the most. Because I get a lot of information via hard copy publications too and I have some subscriptions, I periodically take time to read those also.

Amelia: Many of us grew up in school reading front to back, cover to cover, starting at the beginning and reading to the end. Do you find yourself still doing that or do you read small chunks or scan the text and try to pick out what you want?

Shenita: Well, that's a good question. It really depends what we're talking about. If we're talking about a magazine, for instance a human resources magazine, I don't know why I do this, but I usually go from back to front. I scan first then I look at the table of contents and then I usually choose one or two articles. Then I'm done with that publication.

Amelia: It sounds like you are selectively reading. You're kind of scanning through until you find something. Is that a good way to describe it?

Shenita: Yes, I had to learn that when I was getting my doctorate as a time saver. I focus on things that interest me and keep up on best practices.

Amelia: Let's go back to that. When you were getting your doctorate, or even your master's for that matter, it sounds like you trained yourself to scan through and only focus on what was important, so you didn't have to read 2,000 pages a week. So when you're doing that, how do you determine what parts are important and what parts you can skip?

Shenita: So if I'm reading, let's take a journal for instance, if I'm looking at the latest journal, I usually pick it up with something in mind. If I don't have something in mind, I look for a trend, best practice, or for something else that interests me. . . . If it's something I want to know about, if it's a subject area that I don't have a lot of knowledge in, I'm always zeroing in on that as a second tier of reading.

Amelia: So let's say you've encountered something new to you as you're reading along. How do you take that in, comprehend it, and learn it? Do you look for connections? Do you think "This kind of sounds like something I know about already"? How do you link information together?

Shenita: I'm looking across the spectrum of what I do. I manage the employee experience from entry into the organization to exit. So I'm a subject matter expert across six functional areas. I have one or two areas where I don't know as much as I do in the other areas. I try to zero in on, for instance, executive compensation. So if there's something about executive compensation, I can learn and connect to it. What I do is try to read the information and then I ask myself, "What can I take from this piece that I just read and apply to the structure where I currently work? Is it applicable? How could I modify it so that it's applicable in this environment or so I can incorporate it or relate it to any other function?" That's how I think about things. It's almost like a puzzle. I see what I read as a piece and what I do is the puzzle. And then I look at what I'm reading and I say, "Where does this particular piece fit into the larger puzzle?" That's how I try to integrate it into the work. And sometimes it's just a very good idea that I have to put on the shelf. But, for whatever reason, the retention of those shelf items or parking lot items is very high for me. Periodically, I say, "I remember reading blah, blah, blah. This is where that particular thing could fit in."

Amelia: It's interesting to hear you say that because I do the same thing with educational pieces. Even if it's not in my content area, I think, "How can I adapt this to make it fit for me?"

Shenita: Exactly. That's how I do it.

Amelia: How often is reading required in your profession? Do you read every day? Every week? Is it a once-a-month thing?

Shenita: Every day, several times a day, whether it's a short memo, whether it's an instruction. Already today I have five things that I have to read, and one is pretty substantial. We're getting ready for an audit. Well, two things, an audit and we're participating in a survey.

Amelia: An audit can be pretty rigorous. Can you just read that kind of material through and comprehend it or do you have to use some type of strategies with more heavy-duty reading? Do you underline or take notes? How do you manage all that information?

Shenita: What I try to do is break it up into subject matter. This particular audit deals with one of those functional areas I talked about earlier. So, I would try to organize material based on content within that functional area. There's always a strategy. I'm always trying to manage my time. I'm always trying to solve a problem or answer a question. Or just really get ahead of the assignment in a way that's strategic.

Amelia: If there are students in college right now who are not proficient readers, could they be successful in your profession? Are they going to be able to handle the reading it requires?

Shenita: Absolutely. I think that it first starts with desire and passion. If you have an interest, let that interest fuel your desire to do better and better. I started off as a person who did not like to read at all and then I started to see the benefits of it. It improves your vocabulary. It helps you understand things that you knew nothing about. It exposes you to a world of information. I am a very curious person by nature. So, I cannot maintain my curiosity without reading. I can't understand things without reading and making that connection. Reading can further your career. It can help you do a deep dive into content. There are just so many benefits to it. When I started to figure out the strategies, I said, "This is not so bad." I realized I didn't need to read every single word. I learned that in graduate school. You don't have to read every single word. Then you develop strategies for how to whittle down the information into bite-size pieces.

Amelia: So, you're just looking at what's important, not at the whole thing?

Shenita: Correct. Every now and then, when I have the time, I'll look at the whole thing. But that's only with things I do as hobbies, those kinds of things.

APPENDIX

"Four Parenting Styles and How They Influence Child Behavior" by Kendra Cherry

Parents clearly have an influence on their children, but the question of exactly how and to what degree parenting behaviors and practices influence child development has fascinated psychologists for years. Consider how siblings raised in the same home can have such varied personalities and outcomes as adults. On the other hand, children raised in dramatically different environments can end up being remarkably similar to each other despite their dissimilar backgrounds.

While the debate over the relative role of nature and nurture will no doubt continue for years to come, researchers have uncovered considerable evidence pointing to the effects of different styles of parenting. During the mid-1960s, psychologist Diana Baumrind conducted an investigation into the parenting styles with over a hundred preschool-aged children.

Based on her research, which included naturalistic observations as well as parental interviews, she concluded that there were four key dimensions that shaped parenting:

- **Parental control:** how consistently the rules are enforced, how persistent the parent is in gaining the child's compliance, and the amount of structure provided by the parent

- **Demands for maturity:** the parent's expectations of the child in terms of self-regulation and self-control
- **Communication style:** how the parent communicates feelings, expectations, and demands including whether they ask children for opinions and whether they explain the reasoning behind these guidelines
- **Nurturance and warmth:** the level of nurturance provided by the parent including protections for the child's emotional and physical safety

Baumrind then outlined three basic styles of parenting that contribute to child development and behavior. During the 1980s, psychologists Maccoby and Martin conducted additional research that led to the addition of a fourth style of parenting.

It is important to note that parenting styles are more than just sets of parenting practices. Instead, they reflect an overall attitude and approach to how children are socialized and these styles have been shown to reliably predict cognitive, social, and emotional functioning both now and later in life.

The Characteristics and Effects of Parenting Styles

Authoritative Parenting:

Authoritative parents have clear rules and guidelines for their kids, but they are also responsive and willing to explain the reasoning behind the rules. They listen to their kids, but are not punitive or rejecting when their children make mistakes. Baumrind suggested that these parents are supportive and monitor their children's behavior carefully in order to offer boundaries and feedback without being intrusive or restrictive.

Experts tend to agree that authoritative parenting is the overall best approach that produces children who are capable, happy, self-confident, and successful.

Authoritarian Parenting:

Authoritarian parents have strict rules that they expect to be followed without question or explanation. Breaking the rules usually results in punishment. These parents expect perfect obedience and have high demands, but are not responsive to their children.

The authoritarian approach typically results in kids who are obedient, but lack self-esteem and social competence.

Permissive Parenting:

Permissive parents have few rules and demands. They do not discipline their children because they have very low expectations for self-control. They do tend to be responsive to their children's needs and communicate with their kids, but they often take on a role of a friend more than that of a parent.

As a result, these children tend to have very poor self-control, often do poorly in school, and may have difficulty with authority figures.

Uninvolved Parenting:

These parents provide basic survival needs for their children, but are generally very detached and offer little in terms of love, support, and communication. They make few if any demands of their children, and some may even neglect or reject their kids.

This style results in the worst outcomes across all areas including emotional, cognitive, and social development. Kids raised by uninvolved parents tend to have low social competence, low self-esteem, and poor self-regulation.

How Do Parenting Styles Form?

If authoritative parenting is the best approach, why don't all parents just use this style? Differences in parenting styles are related to a number of factors that can include socioeconomic status, family size, educational background, religion, culture, family history, and overall personality. A person with a strict personality type who is not good at expressing emotions, for example, is probably much more likely to express an authoritarian approach to parenting. How people were raised by their own parents plays a role in the later development of their own parenting style. Those raised by responsive authoritative parents are much more likely to utilize a similar style with their own children.

The Limitations of Parenting Styles

While the authoritative style is generally touted as the "best" approach by psychologists and parenting experts, researchers emphasize that there is no "one-size-fits-all" universal style that guarantees the greatest outcomes. The authoritative style has been linked to good outcomes in Western cultures, but some research suggests that this isn't necessarily true in cultures outside of North America and Europe.

Of course, individual parents often have very different styles of parenting, so kids ultimately end up being raised in homes where a mix of approaches exists. Mom might be more permissive while dad tends to be stricter and authoritarian. In order to offer a cohesive structure in the home, finding middle ground and learning to cooperate is essential. While parents may not necessarily agree on parenting practices in every situation, presenting a united, supportive, and consistent approach is perhaps the most important lesson parents should learn.

4

Developing Higher-Level Questions

The art and science of asking questions is the source of all knowledge.

—Thomas Berger

Professional Spotlight

Figure 4.1.

I'll read some things, then see something that catches my eye, something I find interesting, then I strategize. "Okay, how do I want to put that in my magazine in a way that will make it interesting for my readers?" Then I execute that strategy. It's important to me to go about it that way.

Scott Costa, Magazine Publisher

Chapter 4

Reasonable question: How can I get my students to interact more deeply with the texts I assign, to actually want to know what's in them?

One of the basic foundations of effective teaching is asking good questions, ones that require students to give more than simple "yes" or "no" responses, ones that require them to move from lower levels of thinking to higher levels of thinking. Just as students need to be challenged with such higher-level questions as they learn from an instructor, they need to be challenged to develop such questions for themselves as they read.

Reading is a skill that requires more than visually processing words. It requires mentally processing words, making meaning out of them, and then thinking critically about that meaning. When we ask questions as we read, we are not only taking in information; we are actively engaged in constructing knowledge from that information (Lewin 2010).

Students who learn to effectively interact with a text on this level will not only be better readers; they will be better thinkers. They will be more able to clarify their initial thinking about a text, decide on important information to look for as they read, and stay more critically engaged as they look for and then process that information.

Most students, especially struggling readers, do not naturally ask higher-level questions when they are reading. Many don't ask any questions at all, or if they do, their questions are of the flat, surface-level variety, which do little to promote critical thinking.

This will become clear the first time students are asked to jot down questions in the margins as they think through a text. Responses will typically consist of one or two words at best. For instance, one student might write "Why?" Another might expand his question to "What's this?" Clearly these students do not know how to develop questions that are beyond the most basic who, what, when, where, and why.

The skill of asking higher-level questions as they read is not something students are going to easily pick up on their own once they get to college. It is a skill we are going to have to teach them.

USING FOCUS QUADRANTS TO
TEACH QUESTIONING STRATEGIES

One highly effective way to teach students to ask higher-level questions as they read is to use an activity called Focus Quadrants that taps into their strengths as visual learners.

The current generation is continually immersed in a flood of visual images, especially via the Internet. They are not only receiving this flood; they are helping to produce it. With cameras in their phones, students can take "pics" and post them in a microsecond. This is now a common, everyday way of communicating that previous generations would have never imagined.

We can capitalize on this when teaching students how to develop higher-level questions. If they learn how to ask such questions about what they see, they can learn how to ask similar questions about what they read.

The first step is finding a visual image to use. The image can be related to an instructor's content area but does not necessarily have to be. The key is to choose one that will provoke thought in students. The image used here as an example is a photograph titled "Music of Love" by photographer Ario Wibisono (figure 4.2). Several sources of other effective images are listed in the Toolbox at the end of this chapter.

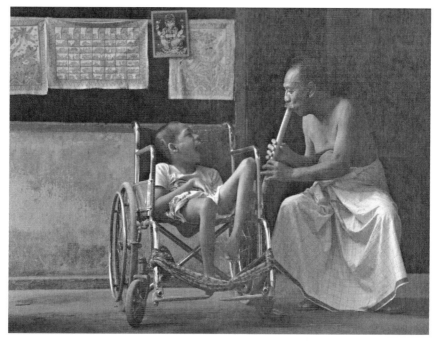

Figure 4.2.

Begin by displaying the image in front of the class. It is best to use a document camera or some other device that provides the ability to write on the margins of the image either by hand or electronically.

Give students a few minutes to study the photograph and then ask, "What are some questions people might have about this picture?" As the students begin developing and sharing their responses aloud, record them on the doc cam.

The following are some questions students typically ask about the photo: Where are they? Are the man and the boy related? What kind of instrument is the man playing? What's wrong with the boy? What's hanging on the wall in the background?

Before long, students will run out of surface-level questions. At this point, remove the photo and the students' questions from the doc cam and put up a blank piece of paper. Quickly draw a quadrant and label the four spaces with the following titles: social, educational, cultural, and scientific (figure 4.3). Then, put the photo back up and ask students, "What questions do you have about the picture that might be related to social issues?"

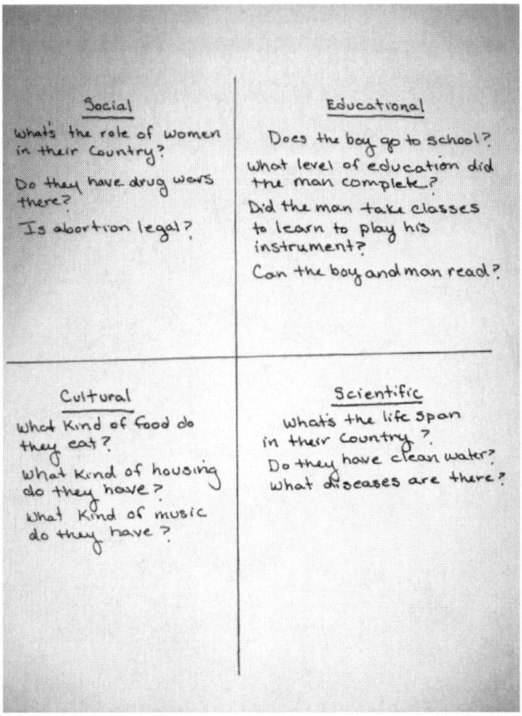

Figure 4.3.

Let the students study the photo again. If needed, offer a sample question to help them, such as "What are the roles of women in this country?" As students share their own questions, write them in the quadrant box titled "social." See figure 4.3 for some actual student responses.

After several questions are developed, move to the next box titled "educational," and prompt students to develop education-related questions about what they see in the photograph. As students get the hang of it, they will begin to generate more in-depth questions: Does the boy go to school? What level of education did the man complete? Did the man take classes to learn to play his instrument? Can the boy and the man read? Move on, generating questions and completing the last two boxes in the quadrant.

This activity can be adapted for use with any image in any content area. For example, when using a photo of a frog in a biology class, the quadrant titles might be ecological, geographical, biological, evolutionary, etc. A list of other possible quadrant titles can be found in the Toolbox at the end of this chapter.

After you have worked through the four quadrants developing questions, lead students in a short discussion about how the questions they asked at first are different from the ones they asked later. Most students will not be familiar with the concept of higher- and lower-level questions. It will be eye opening for them to realize how the higher-level questions helped them to think more deeply about the picture.

Then briefly talk about how questions like this help us to be not only more effective thinkers but more effective learners because asking higher-level questions engages us in the pursuit of discovering higher-level answers. W. Edwards Deming, a well-known statistician, professor, and international business consultant, once said, "If you do not know how to ask the right questions, you discover nothing." If we discover nothing, we learn nothing.

Talk to students about how the questions they asked about the photograph could lead them on a very interesting search for answers outside the limits of the image itself. What they could discover and learn about society, education, culture, and science would be missed without the questions.

The same is true for reading. Asking higher-level questions as they read sets them on the same quest for answers. And since texts provide so much more immediate information than do images, many of their discoveries can be made right away as they read. The more they discover in the texts they read, the more they will learn from those texts.

Once they get this, they will be ready for a demonstration of how to apply the strategy to reading and then to be given an opportunity to practice this skill independently.

TEACHING STUDENTS TO APPLY QUESTIONING STRATEGIES TO READING

In the Focus Quadrant activity, students were given specific prompts to help them develop higher-level questions. They will not have this advantage as they apply this skill to reading. They will have to learn how to develop questions through their own thinking processes instead.

This will seem daunting to students at first. However, there is a wonderful quality of the human brain that you can point out that will ease some of their fears. That is the natural inclination of our brains to constantly seek to understand the world by asking questions.

To illustrate this, have students think about how many times they ask themselves questions in a day. How many times in an hour? How many times in a minute? Our senses are taking in so much information that we have a constant stream of questions going through our minds, nearly subconsciously sometimes: Who's wearing that strong perfume? I wonder where that ambulance I just heard is going. Why is it so hot in here? What do I want for lunch? What's written on the back of that guy's T-shirt?

We can consciously use this natural inclination while we are reading. The key word here is "consciously." Whether we are fully aware of it or not, our minds are asking all kinds of questions as we read. We just need to slow our minds down enough to consciously focus on them.

A good way to do this is to start paying attention to how many times our brains say, "Hmm?" as we read. It's that little pause right before a question comes. Hmm? What does that mean? Hmm? Why would they say that? Hmm? How does that work?

Once we start noticing when our brains pause to say "hmm?" we can pause to consciously focus on the question that is coming. For instance, if we are reading an article about homelessness and read that it is a rapidly growing problem among younger military veterans, our brains are likely to say, "Hmm, I wonder why that is?" We can then focus on that question by jotting it down.

These questions then become what Harvard University's web document, "Interrogating Texts," calls "reminders of the unfinished business you still have with a text." (Gilroy 2004). These reminders get us engaged in the activity of interacting with what we are reading, searching out information, speculating, hypothesizing, and constructing knowledge from what we discover.

You can easily show students that this is the same thing they were doing when they asked questions about the picture: "Hmm? I wonder what's wrong with the boy. Are there any doctors in his country who could help him?" A classroom demonstration will help students see how this works.

The first step is choosing a text for the demonstration. Using a piece of short fiction can be very effective because students are generally more familiar with this than they are with nonfiction. If they do not have to focus a lot of energy on the actual reading itself, they will be more able to focus on consciously paying attention to the questions their brains are asking. Once they learn to do this, they can more easily apply this skill to content-area material.

When selecting a piece of fiction to use for a demonstration, choose one that will spur students' brains to ask a lot of questions and drive them to search for answers. One such text is "The Delivery Woman," a piece of microfiction by Rhonda Hurst (full text included below).

"The Delivery Woman" by Rhonda Hurst

The woman stood outside the man's door with a key in her hand. They had lived a long time in the same run-down apartment building, she on the bottom floor and he on the top. Nearly every day for the last ten years, she had gone up the four flights of stairs to his flat and left things outside his door. Groceries, mail, things like that. Two times a month, there would also be a bundle of newspapers. It would show up at the post office all wrapped in plastic and bound with twine.

She had decided that the papers were from places he went on his trips. He was always gone twice a month, and the bundles always came a few days after he got back. She couldn't ask him because they never talked except in notes left on doors. It had been like that since the first day they met.

That had been out on the front sidewalk. He had taken his umbrella to two tough boys who, for sport, had knocked a shopping bag out of her hands. "The powerful must be brought low!" he had repeated along with the blows. Those were the only words she had ever heard him say. When the boys fled, he picked up her things and carried them in. She remembered how he had silently looked around at her place. It made her feel the shabbiness of it. The next day, the first note appeared on her door. He would pay her rent if she would start the deliveries and never talk about the arrangement with anyone. That worked out. No one in the building ever talked to her anyway.

She knew the deliveries had saved her. She thought of that every time she carried things up. This has saved me, she would say to herself no matter how tired she got. The papers made her the most tired. She would have to stop and rest on the third floor landing. It was worse in the summer. The narrow stairwell was airless. There were no windows, and the door to the one fire escape had been bolted shut to keep out thieves. But those newspapers had saved her she'd always say to herself.

Not long after the man left on his last trip, a letter arrived addressed to her in care of the man's post office box. It was from a lawyer's office. There was a key inside and a sealed note from the man.

The note was short just like all the others. He wouldn't be coming back, it said. Not for at least twenty years. Arrangements had been made for her to have his apartment and everything in it. There would be another note for her on his kitchen table.

She put the key in the door, went in, and locked the door behind her. The front hall was long and narrow, just like hers. But this one was lined on both sides with neatly stacked bundles of newspapers. She had to turn sideways to make her way through. She had never been in this flat, but it was familiar, living room to the left, bedroom and bathroom to the right, kitchen down the hall at the end, just like hers. The shades were down. She didn't raise them. She turned on some lights instead. In every room, there were more bundles of newspapers, stacked against walls and on most of the furniture.

She found the note on the table on top of another bundle. There were only two sentences. "Open them all. Start with this one." She got a knife from a drawer and cut away the twine and the plastic. The papers were from Detroit. The headline on the top one was bold. DOWNTOWN BANK ROBBED. When the woman opened the pages, money started falling out, big bills, fifties and hundreds. They fluttered to the floor in every direction faster than the woman could catch them. She opened paper after paper.

More money fell onto the table, the chairs and the floor. She ran from room to room opening bundles. There were papers from city after city, all with stories of bank robberies, and all lined with money.

The woman went back to the kitchen and sat down at the table. The apartment was quiet. She could hear the light over her head buzzing. It would probably quit working sooner or later, like so many other lights in the old building. A toilet flushed next door. The neighbors wouldn't notice he was gone, she thought. And they wouldn't notice if she moved in. For years they had just walked around her when she left things outside in the hallway. She should call the police, she told herself. She was just the delivery woman. They wouldn't blame her. She thought about that for a minute. That's all she had ever been, a delivery woman.

Give each student a copy of the story, either on paper or electronically, so they can annotate in the margins as they read. Begin by talking to students about the human brain's natural inclination to ask questions. Tell them to focus consciously on this inclination as they read and to listen for every "hmm?" pause that happens inside their heads.

Each time they hear one, they are to pause, think about the question that forms from the "hmm?" and jot it in the margin. Then as they continue to read, every time they find possible answers to those questions, they are to jot those in the margin as well.

Model this for students by reading the first two paragraphs aloud to the class, stopping when you hear your brain say, "hmm?" and jotting down your questions and possible answers. It might go something like this: Hmm? Why has this woman been delivering all those things for ten years? Is the man a recluse or something? Hmm? Guess he's not a recluse, since he's been going on all those trips. Wonder where he's going? Hmm? Why do they only talk in notes? Why hasn't the man actually spoken to her in all this time?

Stop here and have the students continue on through the story on their own, stopping for "hmm?" pauses and jotting down questions and possible answers.

When they are finished, let them share some of their questions, answers, speculations, and reactions. The story will provoke quite a list, especially regarding the end. Will she or won't she call the police?

Lead a brief discussion on how paying attention to their brains' natural inclination to ask questions helped them to develop intriguing questions as they were reading and how this same strategy will work with their content-area texts.

Follow this with another short demonstration, this time with a nonfiction piece. Choose a high-interest text or excerpt, preferably one that is not any longer than "The Delivery Woman." One effective article is an editorial from *USA Today* titled "16 Is Too Young to Quit School in New Economy." Other suggested titles can be found in the Toolbox.

Place the article on the doc cam, but also give each student a copy. Let them know you are going to work part way through with them, then they will finish the rest on their own as practice.

Read the title aloud and let students hear you thinking through it. For instance, if you were using the *USA Today* article, you might say, "Hmm? What does the economy have to do with the dropout age? How was it decided that sixteen was the appropriate age for dropping out?"

This will let students see right up front that pausing to pay attention to what their brains are asking works the same with nonfiction as it does with fiction. It will also remind them of the importance of looking at elements such as titles, headings, and subheadings as a way to initially focus on a piece of text.

Take a moment to remind them of how asking questions and searching for answers in a text like this is different from what they did with the picture. There they were limited to just what they could see. In a piece of text, much more information is typically available. This allows their brains more opportunity to actively seek answers to their questions as they read.

Begin reading your article aloud, thinking through it, stopping for the "hmm?" pauses, and developing questions. For example, in the editorial about the dropout age, you would read that President Obama "urged every state to require that students stay in school until they graduate and turn 18." At this point, you could say, "Hmm? How would states enforce this? What would happen if students dropped out before that?" You could then write those questions in the margin.

Continue reading part way through your article, stopping to ask and record a few other questions. For the *USA Today* piece, you could write "How does the dropout rate affect the economy?" and "What are the problems faced by people who don't finish high school?"

It is not necessary to ask every possible question that could come up. This would be overwhelming to students. Instead, base how much you need to model on how well your students seem to be following the process.

At about the halfway point, stop and ask students if they had any other "hmm?" questions come to mind as you were reading and thinking your way through. Record student questions at the bottom of the article. If students aren't able to generate other questions, prompt them along by pointing to a spot where you skipped one of your "hmm?" moments and ask students what kind of questions comes into their minds.

Now let students finish working through the article on their own, paying attention to their "hmm?" moments and pausing to jot down questions and possible answers. Let them know that they will be turning in this assignment. This will give them incentive to work seriously on the activity and will also give you a chance to see how well they are grasping the concepts.

When students are finished, lead a short discussion on how paying attention to their "hmm?" pauses while reading helped them to ask deeper-level questions, search to discover answers, and more effectively comprehend and learn from what they discovered.

Below is a list of questions students have written while reading "16 Is Too Young to Quit School in New Economy." Notice how they differ from the surface-level questions students typically ask.

- What does a diploma mean, really?
- School has always been boring, yet we've never had the high dropout rate like we do now. Why is that?
- How will they enforce making students stay in school to the age of eighteen, and what will be the consequences if they don't?

After you have worked through the demonstrations and given students opportunities to practice independently, it is useful to ask them to reflect in writing about how learning to develop higher-level questions can benefit them as readers. This gives students a chance to think about what they have learned and gives you another chance to monitor how well they are progressing. Some actual student responses are listed below.

- The first thing I realized about reading is that I can make myself retain information very easily by following a few steps. If you ask yourself questions and think about what the author is trying to tell you, you can remember the information much easier than just by skimming like you do normally. Because you have no reason to remember the information, then why would your mind want to remember it? By giving yourself something to question or think about it gives your mind a reason to want to retain the information opposed to just doing it because you have to.

- The most important thing I've learned about reading is that you have to comprehend what you're reading about. You have to understand what you are reading or else it is a waste of time. I also know that you should ask questions while you are reading so that the information will stick in your head so you get it. It also makes you pay attention to what you are reading.

- Before I started this class I thought my reading comprehension was good, but I found out it was only good if it was something I wanted to read about. If it was a school textbook or any other kind of school literature I couldn't remember anything I just read. I would read the same paragraph over and over again and still not have a clue what I just read. The most important thing I have learned about reading is to use metacognitive thinking. Think about what you're thinking about and ask yourself questions about what you are reading. It has helped me out so much in remembering what I just read.

- Today with my experience I learned that it is a good idea to ask yourself questions because it keeps you focused looking deeper into the text and stay on topic. Another good thing about asking questions is that it helps you remember what you are reading because you look into the text and for specific items.

THE BOTTOM LINE

Developing higher-level questions as they read helps students clarify their initial thinking about a text, decide on important information to look for as they read, and stay more engaged as they discover and construct knowledge from that information. When our students learn to read critically like this, they will not only be more likely to want to know what's in the texts we assign, but to actually want to *learn* what's in those texts.

That's why many instructors who have seen the questioning strategies demonstrated in workshops are excited to start using them. Here are some of their comments:

- I loved the idea of using photos to prompt questions.
- I liked the idea of showing a picture to generate questions. I think I can relate it to my class.
- This exercise of using a visual will definitely help me to teach students high-level thinking. Also, it will help me to teach them better questions rather than basic or unimportant questions.
- Teaching questioning has never seemed so easy.
- Asking questions keeps students on task, concentrating on what they are reading.

One particularly vivid comment comes from a high school teacher who wrote, "Asking questions creates purpose and helps your mind wonder instead of wander." This teacher really hit the nail on the head.

Wondering is a powerful force for students to tap into while they read. It creates a desire to know. A desire to know creates motivation. Consider a teenage boy who gets a new gaming system. He will engage in some pretty intense instruction manual reading in anticipation of that green, ready-to-play light.

When students learn to read with questions in mind, they have a need to know, their thinking is clearer and more refined, and they are mindfully driven to find answers. Mindfully driven students. Who doesn't want more of those?

TOOLBOX

- Use course textbooks as a source for visual images. They typically have the most relevant photographs, charts, graphs, tables, and other images in a specific subject area.
- Try other high-interest types of visual images, such as political cartoons, historical documents, advertisements, and paintings.

- Start class with a photo and quadrant as an anticipatory set to spark interest in your lesson topic, get students' brains engaged, and encourage deeper-level thinking.
- Use the questioning reading strategy as a "ticket out the door" activity at the end of class.
- Have students keep a journal throughout the course to see how their questions become deeper and more thoughtful over time.
- Take advantage of the host of visual images on the Internet. Here are some helpful links with visuals for various content areas:
  National Geographic Gallery: http://photography.nationalgeographic
    .com/photography/ photogalleries/
  Life Magazine: http://life.time.com
  Science Photo Library: http://www.sciencephoto.com
  Mathematical Association of America: https://www.maa.org/Found
    Math/
  Economics In Pictures: http://www.economicsinpictures.com
  Google Images: https://www.google.com/imghp?hl=en&tab=wi
- Avoid making an expensive color copy of a photo or visual image to display on a doc cam if you have a computer and projector available. Simply project the image from the computer directly to a screen. This will save time too, since you won't have to make copies ahead of class.
- If students have e-readers or other e-devices, have them access photos or visual images via designated Internet sites.
- If there is a particular area, goal, objective, or concept students need to know for assessment or for linking new ideas together, focus on those issues when selecting photos or other visual images and quadrant box titles. Below is a list of possible quadrant titles for different classroom needs:

Biological	Environmental	Occupational
Chemical	Ethical/Moral	Physiological
Criminal	Functional	Political
Cultural	Generational	Psychological
Ecological	Historical	Social
Economical	Industrial	Statistical
Educational	Mathematical	Survival
Emotional	Medical	Technological

- Divide the class into small groups. Provide each group with a different visual image and a quadrant. Instruct them to develop image-appropriate box titles and record their questions in each box. Have students present their work to the class when finished.
- Use double-entry journals to encourage students to develop questions and search for answers. Have students draw a line down the middle of a piece of paper to create two columns. As students move through texts, have them record their questions in the right-side column and the words or phrases that prompted those questions in the left-side column. When the reading is complete, have students look back at their questions and decide if the author answered them. If so, students should note the paragraph or line numbers where the answers can be found. If not, students should write out suggested answers of their own. Examples of double-entry journals can be viewed on Google Images.
- As a mini-lesson, provide a title and some headings and subheadings from a text and have students use them to generate a list of higher-level questions about that text. This can be done as an independent activity or in groups. Group work has the advantage of giving students the opportunity to see the thinking and questioning processes of their peers.
- Access the following texts to demonstrate questioning strategies: "Vaccination Nation" by Chris Mooney and "Experiencing Math Anxiety May Be Like the Experience of Physical Pain" by John Timmer.

PUTTING IT TO WORK

Below is a photo example along with quadrant box title suggestions and sample questions. Though they are specific to a biology class, they will give any content-area instructor an idea of how to put a demonstration together.

Example photo

Figure 4.4.

Quadrant example:

Photosynthesis

Environmental
How does the process of
photosynthesis tie in with current
environmental issues?

Physiological
How does photosynthesis contribute to
the life of human beings?

Political
What steps can the government take
to ensure sustainability of woodlands?

Biological
How can the energy of photosynthesis be
harnessed to aid in cell growth or
development?

Figure 4.5.

PROFESSIONAL SPOTLIGHT READING INTERVIEW
WITH SCOTT COSTA

Title: Publisher
Location: St. Louis, Missouri

Amelia: Can you begin by describing your professional position?

Scott: Publisher of *tED Magazine*, which is the industry magazine for electrical distribution, basically electrical manufacturing for people who make electrical products, and we represent distributors who act as the middle man to get it from the manufacturer to the hands of contracted people who actually do the work.

Amelia: What did you do before you were a publisher?

Scott: Before that I worked in television news for twenty-seven years at a variety of TV stations around the country from California to Atlanta to Columbus, Ohio. I've been in St. Louis for about the past twenty years before I switched over to the magazine side.

Amelia: In your profession now, what types of things do you generally read?

Scott: Well, I'm trying to stay ahead of the industry, what's going on. I read a number of publications that come out from distributors and from manufacturers of electrical products. They publish new products that will be coming out or new strategies, so I'm usually following that fairly closely. In addition to that, I'm monitoring other magazines throughout the industry to see what they're doing or how they're covering specific stories. And then I'm reading just magazines in general. Some of them are news related, some of them are sports related, some of them are entertainment related, to kind of get ideas about what their strategies are to see if I can adapt them to fit my strategies towards making our magazine more entertaining or easier to read. So, there's a pretty wide range of reading that I do on a regular basis just so I stay ahead of the curve on what's new, what's hot, what's next.

Amelia: Do you read on a daily basis in your job? A weekly basis?

Scott: Definitely a daily basis.

Amelia: What is the average length of time you spend reading this material?

Scott: If I'm just looking at the layout strategies of other magazines, the length is fairly short. It might be anywhere from fifteen minutes to forty minutes. If I'm reading actual stories, such as about lighting manufacturers who are coming out with a new product and why, I'll read entire articles that may take me more than an hour. I may read a couple of them. LED lighting is really hot right now, so I'll read maybe an hour a day for four straight days about whatever is new and happening in LED lighting. So, it just depends on what I'm reading for. If it's just layout strategies, it won't be a lot of time, but if I'm looking at new products or what companies are doing, it's usually longer than that.

Amelia: In your profession, it sounds like you couldn't get by without strong reading skills.

Scott: Right, no way. I think of it as more research than just reading. I'm a big believer in research, strategize, and execute. I'll read some things then see something that catches my eye, something I find interesting, then I strategize. "Okay, how do I want to put that in my magazine in a way that will make it interesting for my readers?" Then I execute that strategy. It's important to me to go about it that way.

Amelia: So you think of reading as research?

Scott: I do. If I'm looking at other people's trade publications or if I'm looking at other people's magazines, I refer to that as the research side of things. I'm forming opinions or I'm creating ideas for an editorial or what-ever it might be based on the things I'm reading from other publications or online. From there, I may call a few people into a room and say, "Okay, LED lighting looks to be blowing up here, and there seems to be a wide block of interest in it. Here are a couple of story ideas I think we should do." Then we'll strategize about how we want to do those kinds of thing, whether it will be in our online version or whether it will be in the actual magazine. Then we'll execute that. As a result of those three things, what you usually end up with is a fairly solid magazine that people want to read because you didn't just throw darts at a dartboard. I consider the reading part as research in terms of what stories I should be doing and how I should be doing them.

Amelia: So, how did you become such a proficient reader? Did you have a great public school education? What helped you become skilled at reading?

Scott: In public school, there were a few teachers here and there who were instrumental in getting me to read. To be honest, it was bosses I had when I got out of college and went into the professional world who were like

"Hey, you can't not be well-read because there are going to be other people younger than you who understand stuff more than you do." I have clipped articles from magazines, newspapers, or publications and handed them on to my editors or my writers. I want them to read it and really get something out of it, form some opinions and come back to me and say, "We should do stories on this" or "I found that really interesting and it would be great if we could do something that would make the magazine better by doing this." I think it's instrumental to say, "I really want you to read this. I'm not giving it to you because I want to waste your time or I want you to spend time reading something you're not going to get anything out of. I really want you to read this and get back to me and tell me what you think, get some real idea out of it." I hope college professors aren't just saying, "Our assigned reading for this semester is this book." When students ask why, they say, "I don't know. Because we had to pick a book to read so we picked this." I hope they say, "I'm giving you this book because I really want to get something out of you that came from what's inside of this book." And I hope that inspires students to say, "Ok, I'm going to read this and I'm really going to think about it."

Amelia: What was your college reading experience like? It sounds like you might not have learned the value of reading as much in college as you did later in the workplace.

Scott: That would be true. When I got a syllabus from a college professor with assigned reading, from an English class or journalism class, I always thought, "Why are we reading this book? Is it just so some professor can say students are reading it or are we really supposed to get something out of it?" I never really felt like I got an answer. When I entered the professional world, it became "Hey, I'm giving you this newspaper article or I'm giving you this book to read because it has some real value, and I really need you to focus on it." I just got more out of it professionally when it came to, "I need feedback from you in a reasonable amount of time about what I'm handing you to read."

Amelia: You sound like a busy person who does a lot of reading. How do you determine what's important? How do you determine what to really focus on?

Scott: A lot of times, it's subject matter. There's a variety of topics now that our magazine is really focused on. So, I'm constantly trying to read up on those topics. I'll flip through somebody else's magazine to see if they did anything on it, or I'll do a Google search on those things because I want to know more about them. I'm not reading everything I can get my hands on. Sometimes it's very focused on what topics seem to be hot right now.

Amelia: What percent of the material you read for your profession is online compared to hard copy?

Scott: You know that's a tough one. I would say a little more than 50 percent, maybe 60/40 online. Just about everybody now who is publishing a magazine is publishing some kind of online version. I still enjoy sitting in my office when a magazine arrives and leafing through it, but I would probably say 60 percent of the time I'm reading something online. About 40 percent is a physical book or physical magazine or something like that.

5

Making Connections

Inference is a statement about the unknown made on the basis of the known.

—S. I. Hayakawa

Professional Spotlight

Figure 5.1.

I read something daily. I'm also in a career development program with online journals and books. So I do a lot of that reading as well. I also read different books on my own for professional development.

Don Murphy Jr., Insurance Agent

Chapter 5

Reasonable question: Why do my students read what I assign but never seem to make the connections they need to understand it?

Making connections that link ideas together while reading is a higher-level thinking skill students need to be able to get the most out of college-level texts. This goes beyond simply reading through information. It requires *thinking* through information, analyzing it, synthesizing it, digesting it.

Three important ways strong readers create connections are making comparisons to aid understanding, using learned information to understand new information, and drawing inferences about what they encounter in texts. Students who haven't learned how to do these things before they hit the doors of their college classrooms will find themselves behind in the game before they ever get started and will need their instructors to help them catch up.

USING COMPARISONS TO AID UNDERSTANDING

When students are being taught new information, a common thing they hear their teachers say is "This is similar to X." That's because effective teachers know that comparisons are an important and foundational way human beings learn. This skill is not only vital when students are learning from a teacher. It is vital when they are learning from a text.

Most readers automatically do this to an extent. They often think, perhaps subconsciously, "I get it. This is like X." However, academic texts are typically more difficult than other types and contain more new information. To really learn from these texts, students cannot just rely on their "automatic" ability to make effective comparisons.

Instead, they need to learn to be intentional about it. They need to connect to the texts by deliberately thinking about how new things they encounter—objects, events, situations, concepts—are similar to things they already know about or have experienced.

We can help our students learn to do this more effectively by showing them how to go about it. The first step is to simply *remind* students of the value of a good comparison. They know this from their everyday experience, but often don't intentionally think about it when it comes to reading their college texts. Instructors can help by using a comparison in class and then taking a few minutes to discuss why it aids learning.

For example, if students are being taught about the force of gravity on the earth's orbit, the instructor could compare the earth to a ball being twirled around and around at the end of a string. The speed of the twirling motion keeps the ball in the air by creating tension on the string. If the twirling slows down too much, the ball will fall out of "orbit" around the twirler. The twirler represents the sun, the ball represents the earth, the tension on the string represents the pull of gravity.

After using such an example, the instructor could talk with students about how comparisons like this help us to understand and to remember new information. The next step is to help students learn to apply this as they read. Again, modeling is needed.

Let's go back to that science class. The instructor could choose a short passage from the course text that talks about black holes being funnel-shaped like whirlpools with the pull being strongest at the vortex (the most narrow part), which creates the power to suck things into them.

The instructor could stop there and help students intentionally try to compare this to other things they are more familiar with, such as a funnel formed by a tornado or a whirlpool created by a flushing toilet. Students could be shown how to make notations about the comparisons for easy reference later as they study for quizzes or tests. This could be done with an annotating function on an e-version of the text or in the margins of a hard copy. Then the class could briefly talk about how making comparisons like this as they read helps them to understand and to remember information.

Sometimes making comparisons is more difficult than this, especially when unfamiliar vocabulary is involved. For example, imagine students are reading about how ancient Egyptians used sledges with ropes attached to haul immense objects, such as statues and stone blocks, across the desert sand. Students might not have a clear idea of what "sledge" means. We can help them by explaining that sometimes making effective comparisons involves first taking steps to clarify the meaning of words.

In the example about the Egyptians, an instructor could show students how to use their e-devices to quickly access the meaning of "sledge." They will easily find a modern definition that describes it as a sleigh-like vehicle pulled by horses or oxen that is used to transport people or cargo over ice or snow. The instructor could then show them how to use that meaning to imagine what an ancient sledge might have been like (much larger, pulled by people, used for very big loads, pulled over sand). This could then be noted in the text, or students could even draw a quick sketch of a sleigh to help them remember the comparison.

Classroom demonstrations like this will remind students of how valuable an effective comparison can be to help them learn and will show them how to be more intentional about making comparisons as they read.

USING LEARNED INFORMATION TO UNDERSTAND NEW INFORMATION

Another foundational way humans learn new information is by building on related information they already know. When we learn about exponents, for example, we build on what we know about basic multiplication. Just like drawing comparisons, this type of learning also happens automatically for students to a certain degree, but must be used more intentionally as they read. Again, modeling is the best way to help them learn to do this.

A good way to start is to show students how to build on information they know from their everyday lives or from being part of shared culture. For instance, if students are learning about capitalism and free enterprise in an economics course, an instructor could help them see how to connect new information to known information by talking with them about what they might know about how local businesses operate. Then they could build on that as they learn about the other concepts.

If students in a history class are learning about the effects of the Vietnam War on returning soldiers, an instructor could lead a discussion on what students know about soldiers in more current generations, like those returning from Iraq and Afghanistan. This knowledge might come from discussion in other classes, the media, personal experiences, or the experiences of friends or family members.

Students can then be helped to see how they can use what they already know about these returning soldiers to understand the challenges faced by returning soldiers during the Vietnam era. Once students see the effect of linking new information to known information, they will be ready to learn how to intentionally apply this skill as they read.

A classroom demonstration with a piece of content-related text is a good way to demonstrate this. For instance, a geology instructor could walk students through a short piece of text about how mountain ranges form or about how earthquakes occur and show them how to link this new information to information about plate tectonics previously covered in class. Students could be shown how to jot down a short list of "plate tectonic" details in the margins of the text and then add brief connections to this as they read along and learn about mountain ranges and earthquakes.

In the same way, a college biology instructor could use a text on how cancerous tumors develop. The instructor could start by leading a short discussion about what students know about basic cell division from their high school biology classes. Students could make brief notes on the text and use them to connect to new information they encounter as they read.

When students are more intentional about linking new information to previously known information as they read, they will be more likely to stay engaged with a text and will be better equipped to effectively learn the material in it.

DRAWING INFERENCES

Students find it more challenging to learn how to draw inferences than they do to make comparisons or to link new information to previously known information. Part of the reason for this is that the act of drawing inferences involves abstract thinking processes that can be more difficult for them to understand. Inferences are also more challenging for instructors to explain.

In a reading workshop, the following question was posed to a group of teachers: "What does it means to infer?" The instructors were eager to share their definitions and did so with articulate certainty. That certainty dwindled, however, when they were asked a second question: "How did you learn to develop inferences when reading?"

After some hesitation, one teacher said, "Well, I don't know."

Another offered, "I don't think I was ever taught how to do it. I just figured it out."

A third said, "I don't know how I learned to infer when I read. I just do it automatically."

The challenge lies not only in trying to explain such an abstract concept but in explaining it to students who often do not "just do it automatically" as they read.

An effective way to begin teaching students about drawing inferences is to provide a straightforward definition of the term and a few easy-to-understand illustrations: "An inference is a conclusion reached on the basis of perceived evidence or from premises known or assumed to be true. It involves reasoning, presuming, supposing, and guessing. For instance, if someone looks into a box that is supposed to be filled with new baseballs and notices that one has a dark scuff mark on it, that person might infer that the ball has been played with before."

As a further example, an instructor might say, "Imagine you are driving home and you notice one of your friends has been pulled over on the shoulder of the road by a police officer. Both are outside of their vehicles. Your friend is standing straight up, with legs together and eyes closed, facing the officer. Both of your friend's arms are outstretched at the side, with one bent at the elbow, poised to attempt a nose touch. What do you infer is taking place?"

Most students will know the answer immediately. The instructor can ask students why the officer wouldn't need to yell out to each passing car, "I suspect this person has been drinking, and I'm facilitating a sobriety test." Students will easily see that passersby could deduce this on their own by using evidence and personal knowledge to draw a reasonable conclusion. In other words, they could infer it.

Talking through a definition and illustrations with students will allow them to see that they are already skilled in the art of drawing inferences, they just didn't realize it.

Inferring is one of most basic things we learn, and we do this early on through such things as repetitive life experiences, relationships, nature, communities, and cultures. Even when we are very young, we draw inferences about the emotions and responses of others through facial expressions, body language, and tone of voice. For instance, toddlers can easily infer when their mothers are not pleased with their behavior.

We infer it's going to storm by the way the sky looks or the way the wind blows. We infer if a dog is friendly or hostile by looking at its stance and sounds.

Students generally relate to these examples. After such a discussion, one student responded by saying, "I've been using inferences all my life. I just didn't know what it was called."

Once students have a basic understanding of inferences and of their own ability to draw them, they can begin to apply this skill to reading. Many will initially be resistant because they are afraid of reaching wrong conclusions. They are more familiar with reading to obtain information that is clearly stated in the text, the kind that requires no reasoning, presuming, or supposing.

Inferences are subjective and are based not only on the quality of the information in a text but on the reader's background knowledge, experiences, or observations. Keene & Zimmerman (1997) point out that inferring "involves a mental process of combining what is read with relevant prior knowledge (schema). The reader's unique interpretation of a text is the product of this blending" (p. 162).

When it comes to academic texts, students are afraid to try to reason out such a "unique interpretation" because they have little confidence in their "relevant prior knowledge." It will take some convincing to help them understand that the ability to draw effective inferences is a skill that is learned through practice. They will get better and better at it the more they try.

They will also need to be convinced that it is okay to be wrong. Inferences are risky business because they are often reached by reasoning through information that is indirect or implied. Scientific theories are actually inferences, many of which are proven wrong after being tested. Where would we be if scientists were afraid to develop theories because they were afraid of being wrong?

An effective way to begin teaching students how to draw inferences is through classroom demonstrations using short pieces of fiction or images such as cartoons like the example in figure 5.2.

When working with cartoons, show only the image, not the caption. Have students look at elements in the image and attempt to draw inferences about what they see. For example, when working with the cartoon below, direct students to notice things like the ages of the men, their positions at the desk, their body language (one leaning forward with arms crossed, one sitting back with arms at his sides), facial expressions, the

*"I'll have someone from my generation get in touch
with someone from your generation."*

Figure 5.2.

cell phone next to the younger man, etc. Then ask them what they might infer from these things.

Students typically offer the following responses. The men are professionals because they are wearing suits. They are in a city, probably in an office building. The younger man is more tech savvy and current than the older man. The younger man is in charge, perhaps as some kind of boss or authority figure. He is more serious, maybe even irritated, while the older man is uncomfortable or dismayed.

Next uncover the caption, let students read it, and then ask them to make more inferences. Students often say that the younger man is speaking and that he seems to be brushing off the older man because of the generation gap between them.

Using cartoons like this can be very effective because students will quickly realize that they didn't reach their conclusions only through what they observed and read. They also reached them through their own knowledge and experience, what they perceived to be evidence, premises they knew or assumed to be true, and their own reasoning, presuming, supposing, and guessing.

The next step would be to do a class demonstration using a piece of academic text. The example below is a case study based on a true situation and formatted like case studies often found in psychology or sociology textbooks. The sentences have been numbered, and sample sections that contain opportunities to draw inferences have been put in bold. Below the text is an explanation of how this case study can be used in a classroom demonstration.

MAKING CONNECTIONS CASE STUDY

(1) Denise was an adult volunteer at a youth activity center when she first met Jody, a girl from a local neighborhood. (2) Jody was twelve years old at the time and had two younger brothers. (3) **They lived with their mother and a series of the mother's boyfriends.** (4) The fathers of the children were not involved in their lives.

(5) **During Jody's teen years, her mother would sometimes go away for days at a time, leaving Jody to care for the two boys with the supervision of an uncle, a single man in his thirties who lived next door.** (6) **The children would often run out of food and miss school during those times.**

(7) Protective services had been contacted on several occasions. (8) When workers came, the uncle convinced them that the children were being cared for. (9) Denise tried to check on the children herself, but Jody wouldn't let her in. (10) **She said her uncle wouldn't like it.** (11) Denise asked if he was staying with them or at his own house. (12) **Jody told her, "He comes sometimes, usually late at night."**

(13) Jody left home when she was seventeen. (14) **By the time she was twenty-two, she had four children by three different fathers.** (15) **She would often call Denise for help with money and food.** (16) **When Denise went to the house, she would find it very dirty.** (17) Sometimes there would even be dog feces on the floor. (18) **The children, all under five years old, were usually very dirty too.** (19) Denise would try to help clean things up. (20) She would also bring in food. (21) **She had stopped offering money when she found out Jody was spending it on cigarettes for various boyfriends.**

(22) **One day Denise arrived and found the children alone.** (23) **Jody was two houses down with some friends.** (24) Denise talked to her when she came back, and Jody promised she wouldn't do that anymore. (25) A few months later, Denise found the children alone again. (26) It was wintertime. (27) The front door was open, and the house was cold. (28) **The children were in underwear and T-shirts and were barefooted.** (29) Two of them had dog feces between their toes.

(30) The youngest, a four-month-old boy, was in a crib in a bedroom on a bare mattress with no blankets. (31) **He was wearing only a diaper, which was wet, and he was crying.** (32) Denise left a note for Jody and took the children to her house and cleaned them up. (33) Then she reluctantly called protective services. (34) A man there told her she would have to return the children to their mother until a caseworker could visit the home. (35) He said he was sorry, but it was hard to remove children without official proof of neglect. (36) **"Show me a broken arm," he said. "Then we can do something."**

(37) Two weeks later, Jody called Denise from the hospital. (38) **The baby had been admitted and diagnosed with failure to thrive.** (39) He weighed only eleven pounds, just four pounds over his birth weight. (40) Denise called the man she had talked to earlier and told him she thought she had a "broken arm" to report. (41) Then she went up to the hospital to sit with Jody.

(42) **Someone from protective services came to the hospital that day.** (43) All the children were placed in temporary foster care. (44) Within a few years, they were all permanently removed from their mother. (45) Jody never found out that Denise was the one who called protective services. She thought it was someone at the hospital.

With the text displayed, work through the first few sentences, sharing inferences aloud.

For example, after reading "They lived with their mother and a series of the mother's boyfriends," you could say, "From this sentence, I infer the mother involved herself and her children in a succession of unstable relationships. I also infer these situations must have been difficult for the mother and the children and most likely had an unsettling effect on the household."

It is best to not only share inferences but to be explicit about indicating the words that prompted them. For instance, tell students that the word "series" led you to infer that there were many relationships and that none of them were very stable.

After working through a few sentences like this, give each student a copy of the text. Have them read through it, stopping after each section in bold to jot down their own inferences on a piece of paper along with the words or phrases that prompted those inferences. Have them put the sentence number next to each of their notations for easy reference later.

When students have had enough time to work through the text, lead a discussion, letting students share their inferences and the words that prompted them. Be sure to particularly discuss how the students built their inferences on their background knowledge and experiences.

Point out also that this case study does not offer an opportunity for students to find out if their inferences are correct. Make sure they know this is okay. Although some texts will give such opportunities as students read on, many will not. That's the nature of inferences. They are drawn on the basis of *perceived* evidence or from premises known or *assumed to be true*.

To give students further practice developing inferences, consider using a very short but powerful fictional piece by John Edgar Wideman, titled "Witness." A link to this story is included in the Toolbox at the end of this chapter.

The concept of drawing inferences is rather abstract and can be more difficult for students to grasp at first than some of the other ways to make reading connections. However, direct instruction along with demonstrations and focused practice helps students understand what it means to draw an inference and to begin to reason through texts to draw inferences of their own.

BUILDING BACKGROUND KNOWLEDGE

The ability for students to make connections as they read is highly dependent on their level of background knowledge. The more background knowledge they have, the better they will be at making effective comparisons, using known information to understand new information, and drawing reasonable inferences.

Students usually have more background knowledge than they realize. They know things about politics, religion, and the economy. They know things about social groups, family structures, and personal relationships. They have learned these things from prior education, work experiences, life experiences, relationships with other people, and so on.

Our culture has also fed into that knowledge through such things as the Internet, movies, television programs, news broadcasts, advertisements, video clips, photographs, newspapers, magazines, and books.

Once students learn strategies to make connections as they read, they become more skilled at tapping into their existing background knowledge. Problems occur, however, when they encounter reading that requires background knowledge they don't have.

When was the last time most people watched a movie or read a book about centripetal force, propinquity theory, or critical approaches to literature? These things are not a part of everyday experiences or popular culture and are often not a part of precollege education. As a result, most students don't have prior knowledge to use to make connections when they read about such topics in college texts.

They will have to build background knowledge as they learn and will need their instructors to help them do this. There are effective ways we can prepare our students for the information they will encounter in the texts we assign.

One is through videos and other visual images. We can either show these in class or hold students responsible to view them on their own. For example, if students are going to be reading about the Civil Rights Act passed in the 1960s, have them watch sections of the *Eyes on the Prize* video series that vividly portrays the social events of that era. If they are going to be reading a novel set in the Amazon, show them visual images of that region of the world.

Another way to help students build background knowledge is through the use of short, high-interest articles. For instance, before students are required to read a textbook chapter on the effects of global warming on third-world countries, have them read a related *National Geographic* article. Or before they read about Lyndon Johnson's presidency, have students read "The Sad Irons," a vivid chapter from a Johnson biography by Robert A. Caro.

Providing experiences that allow students to encounter new things first-hand is another way to build background knowledge. If students are going to be reading about incarceration in the United States, arrange a field trip to a local jail or prison. If they are going to be reading about how local governments function, invite a mayor or county clerk to come and speak to the class.

Background knowledge is essential for students to make effective connections as they read. They will bring some of this knowledge with them when they come into our classrooms and will only need us to help them learn how to use it. Other background knowledge, especially related to specialized academic content, will not come with them. Providing opportunities for students to fill in these gaps will make them much more effective readers and learners.

THE BOTTOM LINE

It is not unusual for instructors in workshops to ask why their students do not seem to make the connections they need to understand what they read in academic texts. Being able to do this requires higher-level thinking skills that, unfortunately, many students do not bring with them when they come to college.

Classroom demonstrations and activities that show students how to make comparisons as they read, how to link new information to previously learned information, and how to draw reasoned inferences will help them to develop these vital higher-level thinking skills.

TOOLBOX

- Use different genres to demonstrate the skill of making connections, such as poems, essays, short stories, or selected sections or chapters in books or novels.
- Content specific suggestions:
  Biology/Medical/Health—*The Origin of Species* by Charles Darwin, *The Immortal Life of Henrietta Lacks* by Rebecca Skloot

Business/Psychology/Sociology—*Switch: How to Change Things When Change Is Hard* by Chip Heath and Dan Heath

English/Literature/Writing—"The Art of Racing in the Rain" by Garth Stein, *Half Broke Horses* by Jeannette Walls, "The Red Wheelbarrow" by William Carlos Williams

Math/Psychology/Sociology/Education—*The Curious Incident of the Dog in the Night-Time* by Mark Haddon

Criminal Justice/Psychology/Sociology—"The Witness" by John Edgar Wideman (http://www.oprah.com/omagazine/Micro-Fiction -Short-Stories-from-Famous-Writers/7)

- Show video clips from movies, television programs, situation comedies, or advertisements and have students practice drawing inferences about the characters and events in them.
- Show students a common image of something related to the subject matter they will be studying in class. As a way to access their previously learned background knowledge, have students brainstorm a list of everything they know or think about the image. For example, a geography instructor might show an image of sand dunes near the ocean or a political science instructor might show an image of people lining up to vote.
- Use cartoons for classroom demonstrations.
  Gary Larsen's "The Far Side" cartoons
  The New Yorker cartoons, http://www.newyorker.com/cartoons
  http://www.glasbergen.com
  http://www.andertoons.com/search-cartoons/math/
  http://www.usnews.com/cartoons
  http://www.sciencecartoonsplus.com/index.php
  http://www.dilbert.com
- Have students bring a cartoon of their choice to class to use as a class demonstration, a small group activity, or individual practice.

PUTTING IT TO WORK

Use the following short text as an overall class demonstration of the three ways to make connections discussed in this chapter—making comparisons, using learned information to understand new information, and drawing inferences. An explanation of a possible way to go about this is offered below the text.

"Classic Scientific Management Theory"

Classic scientific management theory came about in the late 1800s and has had a great impact on American business, especially manufacturing. It is called scientific because it is based on studying work processes to increase economic effectiveness and worker productivity and to decrease waste of materials, labor, and time.

The theory was initially developed in the 1880s by a man named Frederick Winslow Taylor, who began investigating labor processes of that period. Through the 1890s up to around 1910, the theory was further developed and began to have a significant impact on the manufacturing industry. Its influence peaked in the decade leading up to 1920 and then leveled out as competing theories arose. By the 1930s, the popularity of Taylor's theory had faded significantly, but its influence on industry has remained.

A main aspect of Classic Scientific Management Theory is what has become known as the division of labor, in which larger tasks are divided into smaller, more specialized ones. Individual workers perform these more specialized tasks repetitively as steps in a process to develop a product or to complete a project or work assignment. Managers closely supervise workers to ensure quality and productivity.

Factory assembly lines are an obvious example of this. However, many offices, especially bureaucracies, can be organized according to this theory with workers often in cubicles performing narrowly specified jobs overseen by various levels of management.

Whether in the factory or the office, focus tends to be on the organization as a whole rather than on the individual workers. Workers are trained to follow precise directions to complete a task. Independent thinking or decision making is not generally encouraged, nor are workers invited to give input into the company's operation. Instead, managers make decisions based on what will benefit the organization overall, such as policies that will cut costs and raise productivity levels.

Display the text electronically in front of the class. It is also a good idea to give students a copy, either electronically or on paper, so they can follow along and make notations as they go. Since the text is short, read through it entirely with students or give them a few minutes to read it on their own.

After the text has been read, begin the demonstration with a few questions about the first paragraph to help students make connections to prior knowledge. You might choose questions like the following: What kinds of thing are scientists normally thought to study? Genetics? Space? Medical science? What do you know about how they normally go about such study? Did it surprise you to hear that scientists studied work processes? How do you think they might have gone about this, particularly in the late 1800s?

You could also ask students to speculate about the motives of those scientists and what might be inferred about why they conducted such studies. Inferences could also be drawn about the motives of industry leaders of that time who put the resulting principles into practice.

Make a few brief notations in the margins to show students how writing down ideas helps readers think through a text.

Then go to the second paragraph and talk briefly about how the theory developed over time, peaked in influence, then faded in popularity. Help students make connections to other such theories or fads that come and go in similar ways. Discuss what they might infer about the theory from this information.

When you move to the third paragraph, you could ask students if they had ever heard of the phrase "division of labor" before reading this text. Have them access a definition on their e-devices to see how it compares to the one in the text. They could note this definition in the margins.

Ask students if they can think of a comparison to help them remember how workers are described in the paragraph. If they need help, you could suggest something like worker bees or a colony of ants. You might sketch a quick picture of a bee next to that paragraph to show students how to use visual images as reminders of ideas that come to mind while reading.

When you move on to paragraph four, you could ask students what they know about factory assembly lines. This would be a good time to show a few images. Google has some good ones that can be found with the search words "Henry Ford assembly line." Also an excellent five-minute YouTube video, titled "Ford Model T—100 Years Later," can be accessed at https://www.youtube.com/watch?v=S4KrIMZpwCY.

After talking about how the principles apply to factories, ask students about their prior knowledge of offices that operate in similar ways, such as those at hospitals and utility companies. Various campus offices are also good examples that students will likely have encountered. You could also use a few Dilbert cartoons that show workers in cubicles (www.dilbert .com is a good source for these).

Also discuss the word "bureaucracies." Have students again access a definition to bring out the idea that this term refers more specifically to government offices. Have students describe any experiences they have had with being passed from worker to worker to complete some government process instead of having one single person help them through it. Unemployment office? Department of Motor Vehicles? Social Services? The IRS? You could also ask what they might infer from this about the relationship between government and the people.

During the discussion of paragraph four, continue to make notations in the margins and have students do so as well.

When you come to the final paragraph, you could ask students to read back through it and make note of any wording that sounds cold or impersonal. Draw their attention back to the title, "Classic Scientific Management Theory." Ask them to use this title and the wording in the final paragraph to draw inferences about the relationship between managers and workers under this system.

You could also ask students to make comparisons to other things they know about that operate in a similar fashion. Private schools? The military? Have them jot down their ideas as different students offer responses.

It's a good idea to wrap up a demonstration with a short discussion about how applying strategies like this helps us make connections as we read and how making connections helps us learn more effectively.

PROFESSIONAL SPOTLIGHT READING INTERVIEW WITH DON MURPHY JR.

Title: Insurance Agent
Location: Oak Lawn, Illinois

Amelia: Is the reading in your profession required or optional?

Don: Some of the reading is required, but most is not. I have continuing education hours to complete every two years, thirty hours. We also have ethics trainings, those types of things. Some of that's required. I'm one who tends to stay pretty read up on the industry, what's happening with our competitors and how we stack up against them. I also do a lot of personal development as a part of a book club. We meet once a month to discuss the reading.

Amelia: What types of books have you read?

Don: One was called *Breaking the Jewish Code*. We also read a health book that was specifically talking to some of the issues dealing with health in the African American communities. The book that we're reading right now is by Mark Batterson. It's called, *In the Pit with a Lion on a Snowy Day.*

Amelia: Is that fiction or nonfiction?

Don: Nonfiction. It's about thriving when challenging times come up and includes biblical perspectives.

Amelia: In regard to your profession, you said you like to stay current with things that are going on. What types of things do you read to do that?

Don: A lot of it is insurance specific, but I do read things about sales as well. I subscribe to different sales websites that send you articles, weekly or monthly. But I mainly try to stay up on the industry. Say the company I work for is doing something with a particular endorsement on a home-owner's policy, for instance they're raising the rate. Staying up with things helps me to speak to objections or challenges I run into when I'm dealing with customers.

Amelia: So does the company actually give you the reading material or recommend it?

Don: No, not really. That's just something I do.

Amelia: You're motivated to do that yourself?

Don: Yeah, I mean, I want to be a student of the game. To be honest with you, it's one of the things that has helped me to survive. I started my business in 2007 at the onset of a recession. Being well educated and well versed helps me know how to speak to people who call in, to talk about some of the challenges they may be having. Or when I hear something about a certain discount or something another company is running, I'm already prepared for it. When I see things going on with something, like insurance fraud, it gives me some talking points for my staff as well. I have two full-time people and an agent in training. So, there are four of us in the office. I try to make sure I keep them abreast of things going on in the industry.

Amelia: How often is reading required in your profession? Is it every day, every week, once a month?

Don: I read something daily. I'm also in a career development program with online journals and books. So I do a lot of that reading as well. I also read different books on my own for professional development. One I read that helped me out a lot, two years ago, wasn't necessarily industry specific. It was more entrepreneur or business specific. When you tie those types of readings together and you're doing trainings and you're getting coaching from business leaders, online or face to face, it's impossible for it not to make you sharper and better and make you look at things from a different perspective.

Amelia: It sounds like with the amount of reading you're doing, both professionally and personally, you must be an adept reader. I'm wondering how you became so. Did you go to a great private elementary school? Was it something that was pushed in your home? Did you develop those skills later in college? How did you become the proficient reader that you are now?

Don: It was my mother and father. I'll give them credit. They read to us, and they would actually have us read. It kind of became second nature for me. I do the same thing with my children now. Also, I went to a really great Catholic elementary and Catholic high school where reading was a part. We would have book report contests in elementary school. I would win every week. I wanted to read in high school too.

Amelia: Did you see a difference when you got into college? Did you have that same appetite for reading?

Don: I don't think I had much time to do personal reading in college. Definitely not freshman year.

Amelia: How did you get through the academic reading? Were you using any particular strategies? For instance, did you annotate the text with notes?

Don: I used index cards a lot.

Amelia: For vocabulary?

Don: Yeah, that type of thing. Even when I was training to get my insurance license, I still used index cards. While reading an article or reading something else, I'll maybe even write a summary. I'll also go back and reread it again. There have been plenty of books I've read twice.

6

Navigating Unknown Words

We think with words, therefore to improve thinking, teach vocabulary.

—A. Draper and G. Moeller

Professional Spotlight

Figure 6.1.

You just can't gloss over the legal jargon that you don't understand because there's so many Latin phrases that have become Americanized in the legal jurisprudence. You have to know what these words mean. If you don't, you're going to miss the whole meaning.

Gilbert Perez III, Attorney at Law

Chapter 6

Reasonable question: What can I do if students don't have a wide enough vocabulary to understand the reading material in my courses?

Instructors know that students with wide vocabularies gain more meaning from college-level texts. They also know that most students do not have wide vocabularies. This is not only true with content-specific terms but with a great number of general terms as well.

Vocabulary acquisition is not something that happens overnight. It takes years of repeated exposure to words. It is not feasible for instructors to spend hours of class time trying to help students learn all of the words they should have learned before coming to college. A better approach is to teach students strategies that will enable them to decode unknown or unfamiliar words on their own as they read.

One reaction might be to think that technology has made such strategies obsolete. Whether students are reading e-texts or hard copies, they can find the meanings of unknown words with the tap of a button on any number of e-devices. The reality is that this approach is not as effective as it might seem.

One problem is that words can have multiple definitions. Think about the word *field*. It can be an area of land (wheat field), a place for playing a sport (soccer field), a plot rich in a natural resource (oil field), a region of effect for a particular force (gravitational field), a range of perception (field of vision), or a subject of study or work (field of mathematics). One can field a question and field a team. One can also do field work or conduct a field test.

Not only can words have multiple definitions; one definition can have multiple layers of meaning depending on how the word is used. For instance, one definition of the word *haunt* is to visit regularly or persistently. Consider the following two sentences: *Teenagers love to haunt shopping malls. Ghosts love to haunt old mansions.* The basic definition of *haunt* applies to both sentences, but there are added layers of meaning in the second one not present in the first.

It can be especially confusing if words are used differently in different content areas. In a business text, students might read about job applications. In an algebra text, they might read about math applications. Understanding the difference between these two word meanings could take more than the tap of a button.

So, while technology does make it easy to access definitions, students still need strategies to help them think through how to use those definitions effectively as they read college-level texts.

Another problem is that students will not always have access to e-devices or will not always be allowed to use them, such as during testing or other assessments. In these situations, students will have to depend on their own ability to decipher word meanings.

TYPICAL STUDENT DEFAULT STRATEGY

Most students have a strategy they automatically default to when they encounter an unknown word. They skip over it as though it's not even there and keep on reading. Sometimes this won't be a problem because students will be able to understand the overall point of a text without completely understanding the meaning of an individual word. However, many times this will be a problem, a big one.

For instance, consider the following sentence: "Younger members of immigrant families have more of a propensity to assimilate into a new culture than do older members." Suppose students are not familiar with the words "propensity" and "assimilate." Skipping these words essentially makes the sentence read "Younger members of immigrant families have more of a "blank" to "blank" into a new culture than do older members." It isn't difficult to see how this impedes a reader's ability to make sense of the sentence.

When this happens over and over, students quickly get lost in a text. Many keep plowing ahead just to finish a reading assignment whether they are getting anything meaningful out of it or not. Others give up in frustration and stop reading course material altogether.

It is important that we help students break this habit by giving them new strategies to default to instead. The first step, however, is getting students to see the value in learning such strategies.

GETTING STUDENTS TO BUY IN

Students will not care about learning how to deal with unfamiliar words until they understand how much avoiding this will hamper their ability to comprehend information. An effective way to show them is through examples they can relate to.

Choose a topic from their current culture that has a lot of specific jargon attached to it. Then have students brainstorm a list of those terms as you record them in front of the class. Some good topics might be current music, video gaming, and various types of social media. Then lead a discussion about how hard it would be for a person unfamiliar with the words on the list to effectively learn about the topic.

To help students better understand this, give them the following scenario: "Imagine a sixty-year-old woman has a fifteen-year-old granddaughter who moves far away. The woman knows how connected the girl is to different forms of social media and wants to learn how to use them herself to keep in contact."

If you haven't already done so, have students brainstorm a list of jargon associated with texting, instant messaging, Facebook, etc. Then ask them how difficult it will be for the woman to navigate social media if she doesn't understand many of the words on the list and what the woman is going to have to do if she is really committed to connecting with her granddaughter.

Explain how this example applies to students when it comes to college reading. Most students want to leave college with a diploma in hand. Once they realize the important role reading plays in helping them do this, they are more likely to invest the time and energy it takes to learn how to navigate unknown words as they read.

Instructors can also get students to buy in by making them more aware of their vocabulary deficits. Many have been "getting by" for so long they don't have a realistic understanding of how many words, especially content-specific words, they cannot adequately define. One way to help with this is to give students a "quiz" to test their vocabulary skills.

This could consist of a list of words gleaned from textbook glossaries, lists of key terms, etc. Supply a few possible definitions for each word and ask students to choose the one they think is correct. The results will help students have a clearer picture of the gaps in their vocabulary.

Another way to "quiz" students is to display the list of words in front of the class. Have students get out a sheet of paper and use a pen to divide it into three columns. The first column should be labeled "Word," the second "Known or Guessed Definition," and the third "Actual Definition."

Instruct students to write the first word on your list at the top of column one, then move over to the top of column two and briefly jot down what they think the word means. They should repeat this process until they reach the end of the list. When they are finished, display the actual definitions, so students can compare them to what they thought the words meant. Have them jot the correct definitions in column three.

Many students believe they have a grasp on certain words until they are asked to articulate a definition in writing. This can often reveal weaknesses better than other types of assessments.

There is also another benefit. Many students have learned to rely on their ability to guess at word meanings. Such guessing isn't necessarily a bad thing. It is better than simply skipping words because it requires a degree of deliberate thinking based on such things as background knowledge and context. However, some students are weaker at this than others, and it can be eye-opening for them to learn that they are not as skilled as they thought they were.

Easy-to-relate-to examples, classroom activities, and vocabulary "quizzes" are all effective ways to help students buy in to the importance of learning strategies to deal with unfamiliar words in a text. One such strategy is using vocabulary resources.

VOCABULARY RESOURCES

Dictionaries are the most commonly available vocabulary resources. This is especially true since the advent of a wide variety of e-devices that make accessing many types of dictionaries as easy as touching a word on a screen. Many of these resources now come with audio and video features that offer much more than standard definitions.

It was mentioned earlier that using dictionaries without knowing how to apply the definitions is not an effective way for students to deal with unfamiliar words as they read. However, using such resources along with reading strategies can be very effective. The problem is getting students to use dictionaries, even electronic versions. They often view stopping to look up words as just another time-consuming step and opt to skip over those words instead.

Another reason students don't look up words is that they find dictionary definitions intimidating. Take the word "articulate," for example. A student who looks up a definition for this word will not only find that it

can be an adjective and a verb, but that it can be two completely unrelated adjectives and two completely unrelated verbs. This underscores
the need for students to be taught strategies to help them correctly apply
definitions.

A short demonstration can go a long way toward helping students
use dictionaries effectively. Begin by displaying the following sentence
in front of the class: "When we don't take time to look up unfamiliar
words, our ability to understand what we are reading can be severely
curtailed."

Then point to the word "curtailed" and have a few students look it up
on whatever e-device they might have. They will find that it means things
like restricted, limited, reduced, cut down, or decreased. Then ask a student volunteer to quickly explain what the sentence means using one or
more of those words instead.

This is a good time to briefly discuss synonyms. Remind students that
synonyms are words with the same or similar meanings. Tell them that
definitions will often contain synonyms in them or will include a short
list of synonyms students can use to understand unfamiliar words. For
instance, the words "restricted, limited, reduced, cut down, or decreased"
in the definition of "curtailed" are synonyms that help define what that
word means.

Starting the demonstration with a relatively straightforward definition,
like the one for "curtailed," will show students that looking up words in a
dictionary is not always as time-consuming or intimidating as they might
think. This will also prepare them to look at the next definition, which is
a bit more complex.

Display the following short passage and dictionary entry:

"To be elected to public office, one needs to be an articulate person. Voters
want to know what politicians think about important issues. Being able to
explain those issues clearly is a valuable skill."
   Articulate (adjective): 1. Having the ability to speak effectively. *Synonyms*: fluent, coherent. 2. Having joints or jointed segments. *Synonyms*:
jointed, hinged. **Articulate (verb):** 1. To speak fluently or effectively. 2.
To form a joint.

Tell students to imagine they have no idea what the word "articulate"
means, so they have looked it up on their e-device and found the displayed

definition. The next step is to test the meanings to see which one they need.

Have a student read the first adjective definition and the first verb definition along with the synonyms. Point out that these offer the same basic meaning, only in reference to different parts of speech.

Then have students check to see if the basic meaning fits into the sentence where "articulate" is used. Also show them how to look at the rest of the passage to see if the definition fits the context as a whole. They will quickly see that this meaning appears to be the correct one.

Tell students they still need to test the second one to be sure. Follow the same process as before to do this. It will be clear that the second definition doesn't fit into the first sentence in the passage, nor does it make any sense in the context as a whole.

Briefly point out that sometimes choosing between definitions will not be this clear-cut. For instance, suppose "articulate" also meant "to have determination." This definition could fit into the first sentence. Students would really have to rely on context to help them choose the right definition in a case like this.

This demonstration will help students learn how to maneuver their way through dictionary definitions and to use context to correctly apply what they find.

Though dictionaries are the most common vocabulary resources, there are others embedded in their textbooks that will often be more useful to students when they are reading material specific to a content area. These can be shown to students in a relatively simple classroom demonstration as well. To do this, display the course text(s) in front of the class. This can be done using e-versions or hard copies displayed on a doc cam, Smart Board, etc. Walk students through resources, such as glossaries, lists of key terms, and indexes.

Many students, especially those just coming out of high school, need to be reminded that most college textbooks contain such things. It is especially helpful to show them that glossaries and lists of key terms include words not only necessary to understand content in a specific textbook but in other texts students might read in a course as well.

It is also helpful to explain how indexes can be used to find meanings of unfamiliar content-related terms. For instance, if they encounter an unknown word in chapter six, they can go to the index to see if that word is listed as being used elsewhere in the text. Then they can go to the indicated pages to see if a definition is embedded there.

This is a good time to remind students of the benefits of marking up a text as they read. In this case, show them how to jot brief definitions in the margins or to use an app for annotating an electronic text. This will not only give students a quick reference for review later, but the act of writing definitions in their own words will help them more effectively connect those definitions to the concepts.

PREFIXES, ROOT WORDS, AND SUFFIXES

Students will not always have access to definitions and will need to use other strategies to figure out the meanings of unfamiliar words. One effective strategy is to learn common prefixes, root words, and suffixes. While this doesn't sound like a very desirable thing to do, it is an important thing to do. And contrary to what students might think, it doesn't have to involve lengthy lists.

A quick web search will allow content-area instructors to locate good, relatively short ones like the well-known 30-15-10 list. It is concise and widely used, can be easily found on a variety of websites, and includes only the thirty most commonly used prefixes, the fifteen most commonly used roots and the ten most commonly used suffixes.

Some content areas, such as math and science, use specialized prefixes, roots, and suffixes that students need to learn as well. Lists of these can also be found online. Two sample lists are included in the appendix at the end of this chapter.

It is not necessary for instructors to spend hours of class time helping students learn these types of things. They can be required to learn them on their own. However, it is necessary to introduce such an assignment by explaining how knowing these things can help students navigate unknown words, especially some of the difficult content-related vocabulary they will encounter.

Again, this can be done with a fairly simple demonstration in which you display the list they will be learning and talk through a few examples. For instance, students could be shown that knowing "dyna" means "power" will help them figure out that "dynamic" means "powerful." Knowing "hex" means "six" will help them figure out that a "hexagon" is a six-sided figure. Knowing "geo" means "earth" and "ology" means "study of" will help them figure out that "geology" means the study of the earth.

It is no secret that most students do not do optional assignments. If something is important enough to be put on a list and given to students, it is important enough to have some kind of course credit attached to it. This can be in the form of graded quizzes, in-class exercises, online assessments, etc. The point is that if the assignment is to be valued by students, it cannot be optional.

Students will also need guidance to know the best ways to go about studying lists of terms. Below are some helpful suggestions that can be given to them:

- The sooner you review vocabulary or word parts, the more likely you are to remember them. As soon as class dismisses and you leave the classroom, step to the side of the hall and review your list, or as soon as you get into your car or dorm room, review your list.
- You have a greater chance of remembering information if you write it down, even if you throw the paper away.
- The human brain can pay full attention for about twenty minutes. The key is to study often for short periods of time, not once or twice for long periods of time. Cramming doesn't work.
- The last time you study should be right before going to sleep when less stimuli from the day is coming in to cloud your intake of information.
- Vary the way you study from lists. The brain remembers more of what was encountered first, so avoid always starting at the top. Sometimes start at the top and work down. Other times start at the bottom and work up. And other times, start in the middle.
- Tape the list of terms or word parts somewhere you always look, so you have many encounters with the information. Consider putting the list on the mirror where you brush your teeth, on the fridge door, etc.
- Set the clock on your phone or other device for alerts to remind you to take out your list for a fifteen-minute study session.
- Upload flash card or vocabulary apps for quick and easy reviews when you have just a few minutes to spare.

• Use hard copy or electronic versions of index cards. Write or type the word or word part in one color on one side and the meaning in another color on the other side.

USING FAMILIAR WORDS TO
UNDERSTAND UNFAMILIAR WORDS

Another strategy students can use is to think of words they know that look or sound like the ones they are trying to define. These will often be words with common roots, origins, etc. Students can use these familiar words to think through a possible definition for the unfamiliar ones. A short demonstration like the following will show students how this strategy works.

Display this sample sentence in front of the class: "One of the major challenges faced by U.S. senators is the need to prioritize responsibilities, especially those relating to the country as a whole, the people they represent in their home states, and their own family members."

Point out the word "prioritize" and say, "If I wasn't sure what this word meant, one thing I could do is to see if it sounds like any other word I do know."

Read "prioritize" out loud then say, "It sounds like the word 'priority.' I know that if something is a priority it is important and needs to be put ahead of other things." Jot "important, put ahead of other things" in the margins.

Next, tell students you are going to look for any part of the word "prioritize" that you might already know. Then underline the first part of the word, "prior," and the last part, "ize," and say, "I know 'prior' means 'to come first or ahead of.' I also know the suffix 'ize' means 'to make.' So if I put these together, I get 'to make something first or ahead of something else.' This matches what I just jotted down."

Next show students how to replace an unfamiliar word with what they think it might mean to see if the sentence makes sense. In the example, the "revised" sentence might read like this: "One of the major challenges faced by U.S. senators is to decide which responsibilities to put ahead of others, those relating to the country as a whole, the people they represent in their home states, or their own family members."

SWAPPING WORDS

Sometimes the problem is not that students don't recognize certain words or have a basic understanding of what those words mean. The problem is that students don't commonly use them in their everyday speech. This can make the ideas being expressed more difficult to initially comprehend and also to remember, especially if there are several such words in a sentence or a short paragraph.

In these situations, students can swap an unfamiliar word for a more familiar one with a similar meaning. This simple strategy converts texts written with higher-level vocabulary and academic language to a level that is more easily understood.

Imagine students are reading a psychology text and come upon the following sentence: "People often exhibit defensive behavior when they encounter situations they perceive as a threat." Most students would not use the words "exhibit defensive behavior," "encounter," or "perceive" in their everyday speech.

Now suppose students cross out those words and replace them with ones they would say that have the same meaning. The sentence might now read,

act defensively   *are in*
"People often ~~exhibit defensive behavior~~ when they ~~encounter~~ situations
     see
they ~~perceive~~ as a threat."

Although words are changed, the meaning remains the same and the sentence is easier to manage.

This strategy can be especially helpful with material students will need to know for a test or quiz. Revising key sentences to make them more easily understood makes them easier to review and to remember.

CONTEXT CLUES

The fact that students often guess at the meaning of an unknown word was discussed earlier, along with its drawbacks. Guessing, however, can be a useful tool if other resources are not available and if students learn how to base their guesses on context clues, such as how the word is used in a sentence and the meanings of nearby words and phrases.

Consider the following sentences students might read in a health sciences text: "A sports-related injury to a tendon can cause severe swelling, bruising, and pain. While these things will lessen over time, some residual effects might linger for several months."

An instructor could show students how to determine what the word "residual" means by pointing out that in the context it is used to describe effects that "lessen over time" and might "linger for several months." Students could then talk about the meanings of the words "lessen" and "linger" and figure out that "residual" means something that is less than it used to be, leftover, etc.

An instructor could walk students through a few more examples and then let them practice on their own. To do this, give students a brief passage from a course text and a short list of words from it that might be unfamiliar. Have students read through the passage and try to figure out the meanings of the words based only on the context, without the help of e-devices, glossaries, etc. This activity can be done individually or in small groups.

When students are finished, let them share their responses to see how many of the words they were able to correctly figure out. It is important to let them know that this skill takes practice, and they will get better at it over time. Also, though this type of guessing is intentional and informed, it is still guessing, and the nature of a guess is that it will not be correct 100 percent of the time. Students should not rely on it in place of more effective ways to handle unknown words.

Teaching about context clues also provides a good opportunity to remind students that sometimes a brief definition of a word is directly embedded in a sentence. This can be especially true with technical or content-specific terms. An example can be seen in the following sentence that might be found in a social work text: "When a parent's illness is chronic, persisting or constantly recurring, it can have a very stressful impact on a family."

Students often read right past embedded definitions like "persisting or constantly recurring" without connecting them to the words they are intended to define or clarify. When students become more aware of these types of definitions, they can be more intentional about paying attention to them as they read and about connecting them to unfamiliar words.

VOCABULARY PROMPTS

Below is a list of questions that will prompt students to practice the strategies discussed in this chapter. Make this list available to students and encourage them to put it in a convenient place where they can easily refer to it as they read.

- What vocabulary resources can I use to help me define a word (e-devices, glossaries, indexes)?
- What prefixes, roots, or suffixes can give me a clue about the word's meaning?
- Does this word look or sounds like any other words I am familiar with?
- Are there any parts of the word I already know?
- What words from my everyday speech could I swap with other words to make the sentence easier to follow?
- How can looking at the way the word is used in the sentence help me make a good guess about what the word means?
- Are there other words around the one I don't know that will help me guess at a meaning?
- Is there a definition of the word given in the sentence?

VOCABULARY LISTS

Many instructors will find that teaching students strategies to navigate unknown words is sufficient for the needs of their courses. Others might also choose to have students study lists of word meanings, especially in content areas with a lot of specialized terms.

Although there are many schools of thought about the best way to teach key word lists, two things are pretty clear. One is that such lists should be kept as short as possible. Rote memorization of long lists of definitions is not only difficult and time consuming for students; there is also little proof that students can effectively apply such definitions as they read.

Shorter lists of key terms that students will repeatedly encounter in course material should be used instead. This gives students smaller chunks to learn and many opportunities for the words' meanings to be reinforced. The strategies suggested in the section on prefixes, roots, and suffixes are also useful to help students learn key terms.

The second thing that is clear about using word lists is that students must be held accountable for knowing them. Students will not be motivated to learn the definitions if there is no course credit attached. This does not necessarily have to involve a lot of extra grading. For instance, short lists of words for quizzes can be chosen at random from a longer study list. This will hold students accountable for the entire list but make quizzes easy to grade. Instructors can also use a variety of electronic options that automatically grade tests and record student scores.

THE BOTTOM LINE

In a perfect world, students would come into their college classes with wide vocabularies ready to tackle even the most daunting academic reading. In our less-than-perfect world, it would be nice if students just came in with a wide enough vocabulary to make it through an average freshman-level textbook.

Since this isn't the case with growing numbers of students, instructors are faced with finding ways to remediate. The answer is not in spending hours and hours trying to teach students all of the vocabulary they need. The answer is in spending a relatively small amount of time teaching students how to tackle their word knowledge deficits on their own.

TOOLBOX

- Access an online vocabulary or word part learning tool, such as an app that utilizes digital flashcards. There are some great options that include text, pictures, and/or audio, such as Knowji, Quizlet.com, and StudyBlue Flashcards.
- Hold students accountable by uploading quizzes to a learning management system such as Blackboard© or Desire2Learn©.
- Show students a list of terms and model how to identify prefixes, roots, and suffixes to help define them.

• The following activity will show students the value of rehearsal and repetition as a way to learn new terms. Give students a folded piece of paper containing the two word lists below. Make sure the paper is heavy enough that students cannot see the words through it. Instruct students not to unfold the paper and look at the words until you tell them to.

Dollar Bill	Cats
Bicycle	Bowling Pins
Triangle	Football Team
Clover	Doughnuts
Hand	Unlucky
Flags	Valentine's Day
Lucky	Quarter Horse
Octopus	Driver's License

Then give the following instructions:

"When I tell you to go, I want you to open your paper and count all of the vowels on the page as quickly as you can. Count "Y" as a vowel. I'm going to give you forty-five seconds."

Pause to answer any questions, and then say, "Go."

After forty-five seconds, say, "Stop and close your paper."

When they have done that, say, "I don't really care about the vowels. What I want you to do is try to remember as many of the sixteen words that were on the paper as you can. Don't say any of them out loud. Just make a list in your head."

Give students about thirty to forty-five seconds, then go around the room asking students, one by one, how many words they remembered. Again tell students not to say any of the words aloud, only how many they could list. Answers will typically range from zero to six.

Now give the next instruction. "When I say go again, I want you to open the paper and try to memorize as many of the words as you can. This time I'm only going to give you thirty seconds. Everybody ready? Okay, go."

Wait thirty seconds. Then say, "Stop and close your paper. Now make another list in your head of the words you remember."

Give them about thirty to forty-five seconds this time. Then go around the class again asking how many words students remembered. Answers will range from about six to fourteen.

Now ask if anyone picked up on the math-related pattern of the word list. If some did, have one of the students explain it to the rest of the class. If no one picked up on the pattern, explain that each word is associated with a number and that the word is listed on the paper according to that number: dollar bill = one, bicycle = two, triangle = three, etc.

Then give another instruction. "I'm going to give you thirty seconds this time. I want you to try to remember as many of the words as you can, keeping the number pattern in mind. Ready? Okay, go."

Wait thirty seconds. Then say, "Stop and close your paper. Now make another list in your head of the words you can remember."

Give them about thirty to forty-five seconds, then go around the class as before asking students how many they remembered this time. Answers will now range from about nine to sixteen. Just for fun, have the student who remembered the most try to say them out loud.

Next, lead a short discussion about the activity. Start by asking why they did so poorly the first time they were asked to remember the words. Students usually have no trouble realizing that it was because their focus had been drawn to the wrong thing—counting vowels.

Next ask why they did better the second time. Students will correctly say that it was because they were now focused on the words themselves.

Now ask why they did even better the third time. One reason will once again be the fact that they were so focused. Make sure students also realize the roles played by rehearsal and repetition. Their first attempt at memorizing the words acted as a rehearsal making the next attempt easier. They more quickly knew what to do and how to go about it, both when they looked at the paper and when they tried to form the list of words in their heads.

Repetition also helped them to be more successful the third time. They repeated the action of looking at the words, they repeated speaking the words to themselves as they tried to memorize them, and they repeated speaking the words again in their minds when they tried to make their final list.

Make sure students also understand another important thing they did the third time. They connected the words on the list to things they already knew well—numbers. Associating numbers with the items made them much easier to remember.

Shift to a discussion about how what they learned in this activity applies to learning to handle unfamiliar words as they read. First, if students are only focused on getting through a reading assignment as fast as they can, they will get about as much out of that as they did out of counting vowels. Instead they need to focus on comprehending what they read. An important part of this is being intentional about seeking out the meanings of unfamiliar words by using the strategies they have learned.

Rehearsing the strategies will make using them easier and more automatic since students will know more about how to go about it. The more students use the strategies, the better they will get at it. Also, just like rehearsing memorizing the words made students more successful at remembering a longer list, rehearsing the strategies will make students more successful at learning word meanings.

Once students learn the meaning of a new word, the more they repeat that word—either mentally by reading it or writing it down or verbally by using it in their own speech—the more it will become a permanent part of their vocabulary.

And finally, when students connected the words in the activity to numbers, they had an easier time remembering them when they were asked to make a mental list. Likewise, when students connect unfamiliar words to ones they already know well, they will have an easier time remembering the new words the next time they encounter them in a text.

- Use the Vocabulary Chair Game to help students remember the meanings of words.

Arrange classroom chairs into rows, as shown below, each with the same amount of chairs and students. Each row, front to back, will be a team. You can have as many rows as you need depending on the number of students in the class. Teams should be even numbered, so either have extra students take turns sitting out or use them as scorekeepers, etc.

chair	chair	chair	chair	*Back row*
chair	chair	chair	chair	
chair	chair	chair	chair	
chair	chair	chair	chair	*Front row*
Team1	Team 2	Team 3	Team 4	

Give each student in the back row a pen and a stack of scrap paper (large enough to write one word on each piece). Tell students this activity will be a contest to see which team can correctly identify the most synonyms.

Explain that you will say a vocabulary word. As soon as they hear it, all students in the back row will write a synonym for the word on a piece of scrap paper. For example, if the word is "angry," they might write "mad."

Then they will quickly pass the paper forward, in a relay fashion, to the next person up, who will pass it forward to the next person, and so on until the papers reach the students sitting in the front rows. All rows will be doing the same thing, racing to get their paper to the front first.

When students at the front of a row are handed a paper, they should immediately stand up and state the word written on it. The first team with a correct synonym scores a point. If two or more front-row students say the correct answer at the same time, a tiebreaker word will be given to those teams.

After each round, the students in the front rows will move to the back rows and all other students will move up one chair. Then the game will continue. The team with the most points when all of the words have been used will be the winner.

Before you begin playing, explain a few rules. If the student in the front thinks the word on the paper is incorrect, he or she should still stand up and say it and cannot replace it with any other word.

Students are not allowed to give answers, by whispering or mouthing the words to the person in the back row. If they do, their team will lose a point.

If no team comes up with a correct synonym for a word, you will tell the class the answer and then move on to the next word.

PUTTING IT TO WORK

If your students are visual learners or respond well to a more hands-on approach, consider using the following activity as a self-assessment tool to help them be more aware of their vocabulary deficits and to provide them with short lists of words to study. The activity is relatively quick to do and can be repeated several times during a semester using different words.

You will need a list of up to twenty content-specific words along with a synonym or brief definition for each word. You will also need a simple pie chart that has been divided into twenty numbered sections as in figure 6.2.

The image should be outlined in black, have a plain white background, and be big enough for students to write words and brief definitions around the outside edges. There are plenty of places online to access such charts, or you can easily make one yourself. You will need enough copies of the chart for you and each of your students to have one. Each student will also need two different-colored highlighters, markers, or colored pencils. You could supply these or students could be asked to bring their own.

Begin the activity by passing out the charts. Then display a copy in front of the class, so students can follow along as you give instructions. Write the first vocabulary word on the outside edge of section one of the pie chart and have students do the same on their copies. Tell them to write small to leave room for a definition you will provide later.

Once students have all written down the word, tell them to think about it for a few seconds and decide what they think it means. They are not to write the meaning down or say it aloud. They are just to think about it.

Next tell students the synonym or brief definition. Write it on your pie chart next to the word and have students do the same on their charts. Then tell students they are to designate one of the colors they have available as "I know this word" and the other as "I need to study this word."

If the definition you gave them matches what they thought the word meant and they feel confident they know the word's meaning, students should use the "I know this word" color to fill in section one of the pie chart. If the definition does not match what they thought or they do not feel confident they

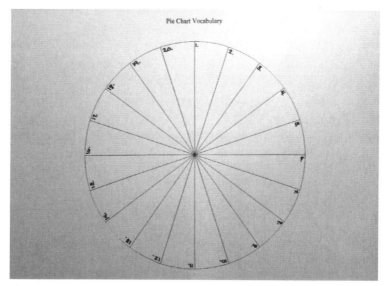

Figure 6.2.

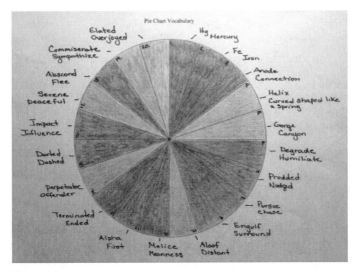

Figure 6.3.

know the meaning, they should use the other color instead. Demonstrate by choosing a color and quickly filling in section one on your pie chart.

Repeat this process with each word. When you are finished, have students look at their charts to see how the colors reveal the gaps in their vocabulary knowledge. Point out how they can easily use the charts and the jotted in definitions to study the words they either didn't know or didn't feel confident about. See an example of a completed chart above (Figure 6.3).

Repeating this type of activity several times during a semester can be a useful way to keep students aware of their need to improve their word knowledge and give them short lists of words to work on spaced out over a period of time.

PROFESSIONAL SPOTLIGHT READING INTERVIEW WITH GILBERT PEREZ III

Title: Attorney at Law
Location: Beverly Hills, California

Amelia: Can you describe the types of reading that are required in your profession?

Gilbert: It changes on a daily basis. The reading is significant. I read persuasive letters from opposing counsel. I read pleas. I read discovery responses. I read motions. I read cases. I read opinion letters. It varies from day to day, but it entails a lot of reading and a lot of comprehension.

Amelia: Are you reading on a daily basis, weekly basis?

Gilbert: I would say daily. I really can't imagine the practice of law without a significant amount of reading.

Amelia: When you're reading is that generally hard copy or online?

Gilbert: You know, sometimes in today's legal environment what I'm reading exists in two ways. I can get it from my legal assistant in online form, so I can look at it on my laptop, but it also exists on my desk in hard copy, so either way.

Amelia: How much content do you actually read? Are you talking about chunks or paragraphs? Are you talking about lengthy letters, or do you ever have to go through actual books or articles?

Gilbert: I don't go through books or articles, hard copies, anymore because everything is digitized now. On my legal database where I do research, everything is online now. But as far as how much, it varies from day to day. But like I said, it is a significant amount of reading no matter what I'm doing. I could read a letter from opposing counsel that's anywhere from two paragraphs to seven pages, but then I have to go back and substantiate what the letter may be saying. So it may be that I have to cross-reference it against volumes of documents.

Amelia: It sounds like that isn't light reading. It sounds like pretty heavy and rigorous reading.

Gilbert: Yeah, it's not light reading at all. As a matter of fact, you have to be able to pick up on the arguments and the nuances. So, it's not just light reading. There's a lot of jargon involved. There's a lot of boilerplate stuff that you have to wade through.

Amelia: So, let me ask you, were you always a good reader or is that something you developed in the field or in college?

Gilbert: You know what? When I went to undergrad, the first thing I did was take an English class that really, really prepared me. In addition to that, I think I've always been a pretty good reader, very able to comprehend what I read and able to articulate my thoughts on paper. But the legal profession is a lot different because the writing is persuasive and there's a certain kind of writing you have to follow and a certain kind of format, so if you think you are a good creative writer that doesn't necessarily mean that can translate to the legal profession. It's somewhat of a learned art.

Amelia: Putting that undergrad English class aside, why do you think you were always a good reader? Was that something in your home? Did your parents encourage that or did you have a great K–12 experience? Were you in private schools? What do you think contributed to that?

Gilbert: I always went to public schools, but my parents encouraged reading quite a bit. You know it's funny that you ask that. I don't have an answer. I guess I just always recall wanting to read. I was attracted to books and reading. But I have never really sat down and thought about how that translates to today. I don't know.

Amelia: I've asked different people the same question. Some think it was their home lives. Others believe it was a good experience in elementary school. There are a lot of schools of thought on that.

Gilbert: I look at the education and the upbringing of my children today and it's vastly different than when I was growing up. There's such an emphasis on reading daily and educational things that I didn't have. So, I would have to say when I was older, as an adult going back to school and starting later in life, I had a voracious appetite for learning and education. I think that may have had something to do with it, awakened something that I had early on but never cultivated until closer to when I was an adult, if that makes any sense.

Amelia: Actually, you're the second person who's mentioned that to me in the last week. I talked with another gentleman in New York who said the same thing. I asked why he thought school didn't work for him the first time. He said he thought he was just too young to be in college. By the time he got a little older, he had a different appreciation for it and, like you said, an appetite to be successful that helped him approach it in a very different way.

Gilbert: I wholeheartedly agree and get where he's coming from.

Amelia: At some colleges, about 80 percent of students come in with low skill levels and are placed in developmental classes, like developmental reading, developmental writing, or developmental math. In the case of students who are struggling readers, if they wanted to go to law school, could they be successful in your profession if they didn't have proficient reading skills? Could they even make it?

Gilbert: Do you mean if we kind of plopped them down in the middle of the law profession at their current reading and comprehension level?

Amelia: Yes. Say they made it through law school somehow, by hook or by crook. Could they make it in the profession if they really weren't adept readers?

Gilbert: They would have to have the tenacity to push forward and make it work. But it would be extremely difficult if not impossible because such a large portion entails just reading and comprehension. . . . So much of my daily tasks include reading, writing and persuasive writing, and articulating and understanding concepts. . . . So, I would say no. I think that goes not just for the legal profession but for any profession where you have to write and articulate on paper. It would be close to impossible to succeed if you weren't a good writer.

Amelia: I've interviewed people from all around the country in various professions, and I haven't had any of them say they could make it if they weren't adept readers. I don't think people realize, or maybe more importantly students don't realize, how important reading and writing skills are going to be, whether you are an attorney, work in IT, are a substance abuse counselor, or work in any number of other professions. If you're going to be in a professional field, you're going to be required to have those skills.

Gilbert: I totally agree. As a matter of fact, I tell my daughters, and anybody who listens, that your written word, whether it be some type of correspondence, your resume, or whatever, that's you in a suit arriving before you ever get there. So when I see correspondence from another attorney and there are grammatical errors or misspellings, I automatically form an opinion about that person based on their work product. If someone doesn't take the time to proofread or has grammatical errors, it says a lot about the person. It says a lot about the work product they're willing to put out, even if it's accidental or they just don't have the capacity to spell correctly.

Amelia: You've mentioned technology a couple of times. We have technology now, computers, e-readers, etc., that can read books or articles to us. I can sit in front of my computer and talk, and it will type what I say and read it back to me. Do you think in 100 years reading will even exist?

Gilbert: Yes, I think it will. Reading isn't just for communicating. Reading is for understanding. For me, I get more from reading than from listening. If you want to memorize something, you read it, you write it, you listen to it. For me, reading is sitting down and taking the time and looking at it, and I process it a lot better than I do just listening to it. I don't think reading will ever go by the wayside. I don't think books will ever go by the wayside either. I myself listen to books on tape sometimes for my commute. That doesn't mean I'm going to put aside the book that you can hold in your hand and smell the pages and you can pause and think about in your mind's eye what the author is trying to convey. . . . On so many levels it will never go away. It goes hand in hand with learning. You can't just learn by listening. Some people just aren't wired that way.

Amelia: When you were in law school and you encountered text that was really difficult, did you use any reading strategies to get through that heavy, dense material?

Gilbert: The first year of law school is like boot camp. It teaches you to think differently. My strategy for that was that I had a legal dictionary. You just can't gloss over the legal jargon that you don't understand because there's so many Latin phrases that have become Americanized in the legal jurisprudence. You have to know what these words mean. If you don't, you're going to miss the whole meaning. Sometimes when you are trying to get through a case and you just want to get it done, it's easy to just skim over it, but you just missed the whole reason for the case. So, for me I had a legal dictionary there, and it was kind of like putting pieces of a puzzle together. I tell my daughters the same thing. When you're reading, there's going to be big words you don't understand, and it's a perfect time for you to have your dictionary there and take the time to learn a new word and what the author is trying to convey as well.

Amelia: When you were using the legal dictionary, were you taking notes as you read or did you remember everything easily?

Gilbert: It's going back so far. I'm guessing I didn't take any notes, but I just tried to commit to memory. I tried using it two or three times thereafter, like within twenty-four hours I would try to incorporate that into my conversation. Granted it's hard to use legal Latin words in your everyday conversation, but ordinarily that's what I try to do. If there's a word that I don't know, I'll try to figure out what it is, what it means, and try to incorporate it into my vocabulary.

APPENDIX

Number Prefixes

Prefixes	Meaning	Example
uni	one	universe
bi	two	binary
tri	three	triangle
tetra, quad	four	quadrant, quadrilateral
penta, quinta, quin	five	pentagon
sex, hex, hexa	six	hexagon
hepta, hep, sept	seven	heptagon
octa, octo, oct	eight	octopus
nov	nine	novena
deca, dec	ten	decade, decagon

Math & Science Roots & Affixes

Roots & Affixes	Meaning	Example
de	down	descend or decrease
dia	through	diagonal, diagram
dyna	power	dynamic
equa	equal	equate, equator
ex	out	exit, exponents
fract	break	fraction, fracture
geo	earth	geology
gon	side	polygon
hydro	water	hydrate, hydroponic
inter	between	interact, internal
intra	within	intravenous
junct	join	junction
magni	great, big	magnify
ology	study of	geology, biology
para	beside	parallel, parabola
poly	many	polynomials
pre	before	precede
prime	first	primer, primitive
therm	heat	thermometer
vert	turn	vertical, vertex

7

Creating Visuals to Enhance Comprehension and Recall

I am a visual thinker, not a language-based thinker. My brain is like Google images.

—Temple Grandin

Professional Spotlight

Figure 7.1.

Reading in my profession requires a lot of comprehension. You then have to take that information to become a resource to your customers, to get that information into their hands, to explain it, to demonstrate it.

Brian Amsden,
Electrical Manufacturing Sales
Representative

Chapter 7
Reasonable question: My students readily engage with video clips. How can I get them to engage that way with course texts?

Our students are living in an age of visual images. Never before have visuals been more prevalent than right now. The numbers of traditional images students see in the world all around them—advertisements, illustrations, symbols, figures, and signage of all kinds—seem to multiply overnight. This is small compared to the tidal wave of images flooding nearly nonstop right into their personal space via television and a myriad of e-devices, including the cell phones they carry right in their pockets.

Not only are students bombarded with images; they help create them. Snapping pictures on their phones and posting them instantly on social media has become second nature. Students also know how to create videos and just about any other type of visual display they can imagine.

More importantly, students communicate with images through such mediums as websites, social networking, and photo sharing. Even when texting, they use emoticons as commonly as they do words.

As educators, we not only need to be aware of the impact visual images have on our students; we need to take advantage of it. Information taken in through a visual image is easier to remember than information taken in though listening to someone talk or through reading words on a page. Since students are used to quickly taking in visual images, using visuals to teach can be very effective. This is especially important when it comes to teaching reading strategies.

Classroom activities involving visual images have been discussed in several other chapters of this book. For instance, using photographs to teach students to develop higher-level questions, showing video clips to illustrate the value of reading with purpose, analyzing cartoons to explain the concept of drawing inferences, and creating pie charts to reveal gaps in vocabulary knowledge.

Using visuals is not only an effective way to teach reading strategies; it is a strategy in itself. Creating their own visual images as they read helps students think through concepts and commit those concepts to long-term memory. Students have been doing this already in some content areas. For example, drawing figures, shapes, and charts is common practice in mathematics. And why is this? Because understanding a mathematical concept is much easier if we can visualize it.

The same is true for all kinds of other information students will encounter while reading in other content areas. A student in a drama class might sketch a couple of quick pictures to help him remember the difference between a proscenium stage and an arena stage. A student in a biology class might construct a diagram in the margins of a text to help her understand how genetic traits are passed down through families. Students in a psychology class might draw timelines to help them remember the stages in the grieving process.

Anytime students are interacting with a text, they have a better chance of comprehending what they are reading. Creating visuals is an especially effective way to do this. It keeps students more engaged as they read and helps them to slow down and think through the information they encounter. Because they can picture their drawings later in their minds, they can more easily remember that information as well. Also, these visuals provide effective study aids that can cut down on the need for a lot of rereading of material to prepare for quizzes or tests.

GETTING INSTRUCTORS TO BUY IN

One thing presenters at faculty workshops learn quickly is that instructors can be a hard sell, especially when it comes to new classroom techniques. Teachers are often suspicious, and for good reason. They have witnessed one educational trend after another, some recycling years later under the guise of a new title. Instructors don't want new trends; they want results. They are clock-watchers, and they don't have time to prepare or to teach strategies that aren't effective. Realistically, only two things matter: Does the strategy work and how much time will it take to prepare or implement?

Let's step into a faculty reading workshop where instructors from all content areas are being shown how to teach students about the power of using visuals to enhance comprehension while reading texts. The goal in this workshop is to create an experience for those attending that is similar to what struggling readers might face with college content-area texts. Students often encounter unfamiliar concepts and vocabulary and have limited background knowledge to help them make connections. In the workshop, instructors will see firsthand how learning to construct meaningful visuals will help students overcome these common reading problems.

The presenter, a reading specialist we'll call Aric, is going to use a short article titled "How Does a Car Engine Work?" The full text is included in the appendix at the end of this chapter. Aric will use this particular article because it is likely the instructors attending the workshop will have limited knowledge of the topic. Working with unfamiliar material will help them to better understand what students experience when they are presented with the task of navigating unfamiliar academic content.

Once the workshop participants are seated, Aric welcomes them and puts a paper on the doc cam that simply reads "Car engines."

Then he asks, "What do you know about car engines?"

Apparently drawing on personal knowledge, one instructor says, "They're expensive to fix."

As several others chuckle and agree, Aric says, "You're right. They are expensive to fix." Then he records the instructor's comment on the doc cam.

"What else do you know?" he inquires of the group.

A different instructor replies, "Car engines require oil."

Another says, "They have more than one cylinder."

As a few other instructors share what they know about car engines, Aric records the responses on the doc cam.

Then Aric says, "Let me ask you another question that might seem off topic, but hang in there with me. How many of you have heard of using visual images of personal characteristics to help you remember the names of people you just met, like connecting the name Rita to her red hair?"

Several indicate they are familiar with this.

Then Aric tells them about a *Psychology Today* blog by Dr. Alex Lickerman (2009) in which he talks about the amazing impact creating visuals can have on our ability to remember things. The article gives a particularly vivid hypothetical example that Aric shares in the workshop.

"Suppose you are introduced to a man named Mike who has large ears. To remember his name, you could picture him clearing out his ear wax with a microphone—a 'Mike.'" Then Aric reads a quote from the article that he has written on the board at the front of the room: "Remember: memory is predominantly visual."

"In this workshop," Aric says, "I am going to use the topic of car engines to demonstrate a reading strategy that involves the creation of visuals."

Then he explains that when students are reading difficult or unfamiliar texts, such as biology, chemistry, physics, or textbooks in occupational classes, they often struggle because they are unable to visualize the concepts. If readers can't "see it," they won't understand it. Creating their own visual images is way to help students "see" information.

As Aric places the text on the doc cam, he explains that he is going to conduct this demonstration the same way he does with his college reading students, so instructors can see how it works. He will begin by making a prediction and developing a purpose for his reading, two effective pre-reading strategies he has already taught to his students.

Aric looks at the text and says, "This is a short article with only a title and no headings or other material to use to make predictions about the possible content. However, since the title is very straightforward, I can easily predict this text will describe how a car engine works."

Then he moves on to purpose. "Once I have an idea what the article will be about, I can determine my purpose for reading. In this case, it will be to learn how a car engine works and be able to remember that information so I can use it later."

He reminds instructors that it is important for students to have a purpose for reading. They need to know what they're looking for in order to find it. One way to have students develop a purpose is to ask them what they want to learn from the text. Their answer is their purpose.

Then Aric adds something most of the instructors are probably already thinking. "Some students are going to respond, 'Nothing. I don't *really* want to learn anything. I just want the credits for the class.'" This brings an expected laugh. Then he says, "When this happens, I give students another way to address developing a purpose by asking, 'What does the author want me to know?'"

After Aric demonstrates making a prediction and developing a purpose in the workshop, he starts reading the text aloud. He underlines parts of sentences he thinks are important and restates, in bullet form, a few types of engines. Not far into the text, he begins creating some visual images to aid comprehension.

Once he has drawn a representation of the injection of fuel in a small space, it igniting and creating an expanding gas (actually just a little box with a teardrop-looking little blob and a few flames shooting out), he stops.

Then he hands out copies of the text and asks the instructors to work through the remainder of it independently, creating visuals to help them more clearly understand how a car engine works. He reminds them that effective reading requires far more than word recognition. It requires the ability to understand the information conveyed by the words, to remember that information, and to use it. He tells them to read with that in mind because he will ask them to remember and to use what's in the text later.

While instructors read, Aric walks around the room, just as he would in his classroom, peeking at their drawings and annotations, conferring and asking a few of the participants if he can share their work when everyone finishes and comes back together.

He notices some of the instructors seem a bit embarrassed when he looks at their drawings. Some make comments about how their scribbles and marks won't be understood by anyone.

"That's okay. It's for you to understand," he says.

When participants are finished reading, Aric asks them to turn their papers over and write a brief summary of what they remember about how a car engine works. "Don't peek at the other side," he says. "This must be from memory."

He can see by their faces they think this will be a challenge, but during the next few minutes, to their surprise, most write clear and accurate summaries.

Aric shares the rest of his work on the doc cam and then asks for a few volunteers to project their work showing their visuals and summaries. Following are some examples of visuals from actual faculty workshops:

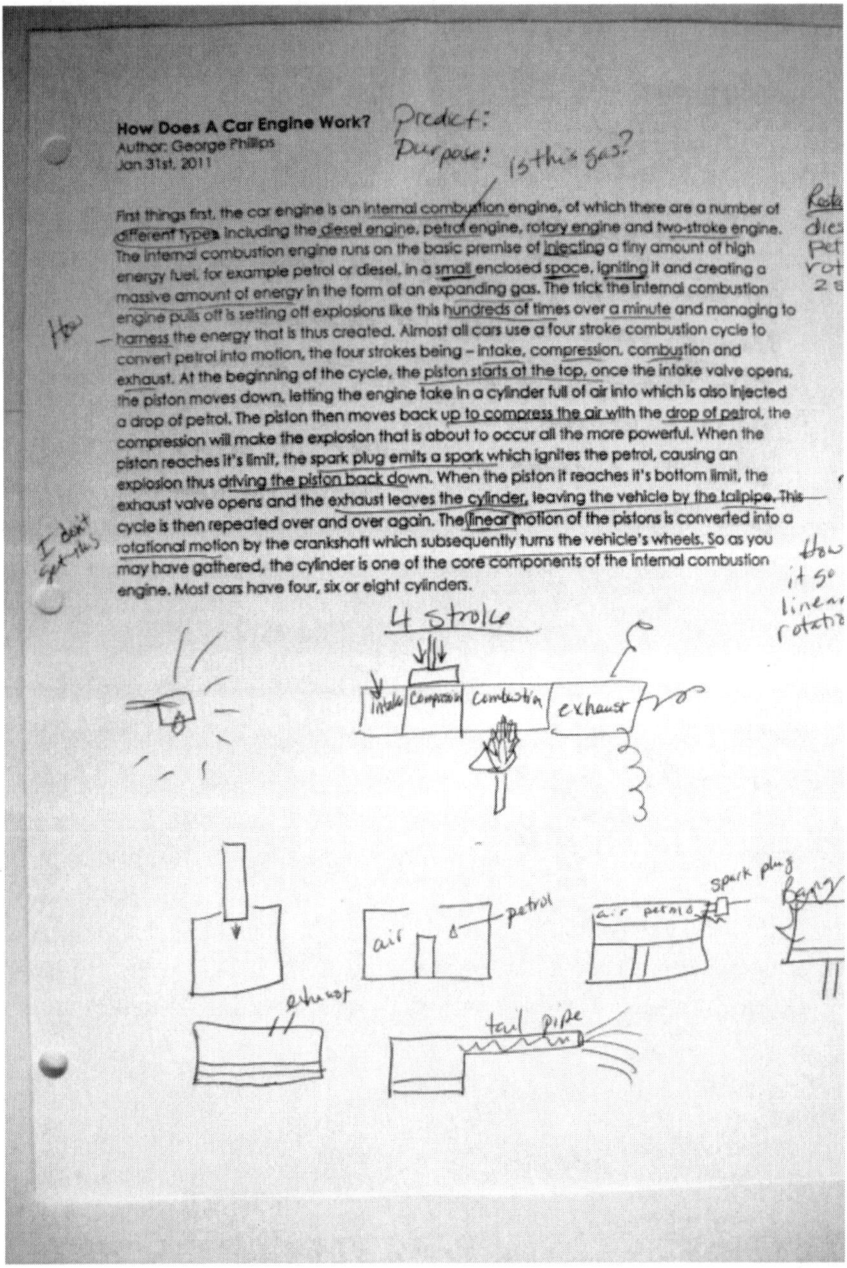

How Does A Car Engine Work?
Author: George Phillips
Jan 31st, 2011

[handwritten annotations: Predict: Purpose: Is this gas?]

First things first, the car engine is an internal combustion engine, of which there are a number of different types, including the diesel engine, petrol engine, rotary engine and two-stroke engine. The internal combustion engine runs on the basic premise of injecting a tiny amount of high energy fuel, for example petrol or diesel, in a small enclosed space, igniting it and creating a massive amount of energy in the form of an expanding gas. The trick the internal combustion engine pulls off is setting off explosions like this hundreds of times over a minute and managing to harness the energy that is thus created. Almost all cars use a four stroke combustion cycle to convert petrol into motion, the four strokes being – intake, compression, combustion and exhaust. At the beginning of the cycle, the piston starts at the top, once the intake valve opens, the piston moves down, letting the engine take in a cylinder full of air into which is also injected a drop of petrol. The piston then moves back up to compress the air with the drop of petrol, the compression will make the explosion that is about to occur all the more powerful. When the piston reaches it's limit, the spark plug emits a spark which ignites the petrol, causing an explosion thus driving the piston back down. When the piston it reaches it's bottom limit, the exhaust valve opens and the exhaust leaves the cylinder, leaving the vehicle by the tailpipe. This cycle is then repeated over and over again. The linear motion of the pistons is converted into a rotational motion by the crankshaft which subsequently turns the vehicle's wheels. So as you may have gathered, the cylinder is one of the core components of the internal combustion engine. Most cars have four, six or eight cylinders.

[handwritten margin annotations: How; I don't get this; Rota, dies, Pet, rot, 2 s; How it so linear rotati]

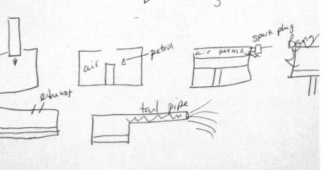

Figure 7.2.

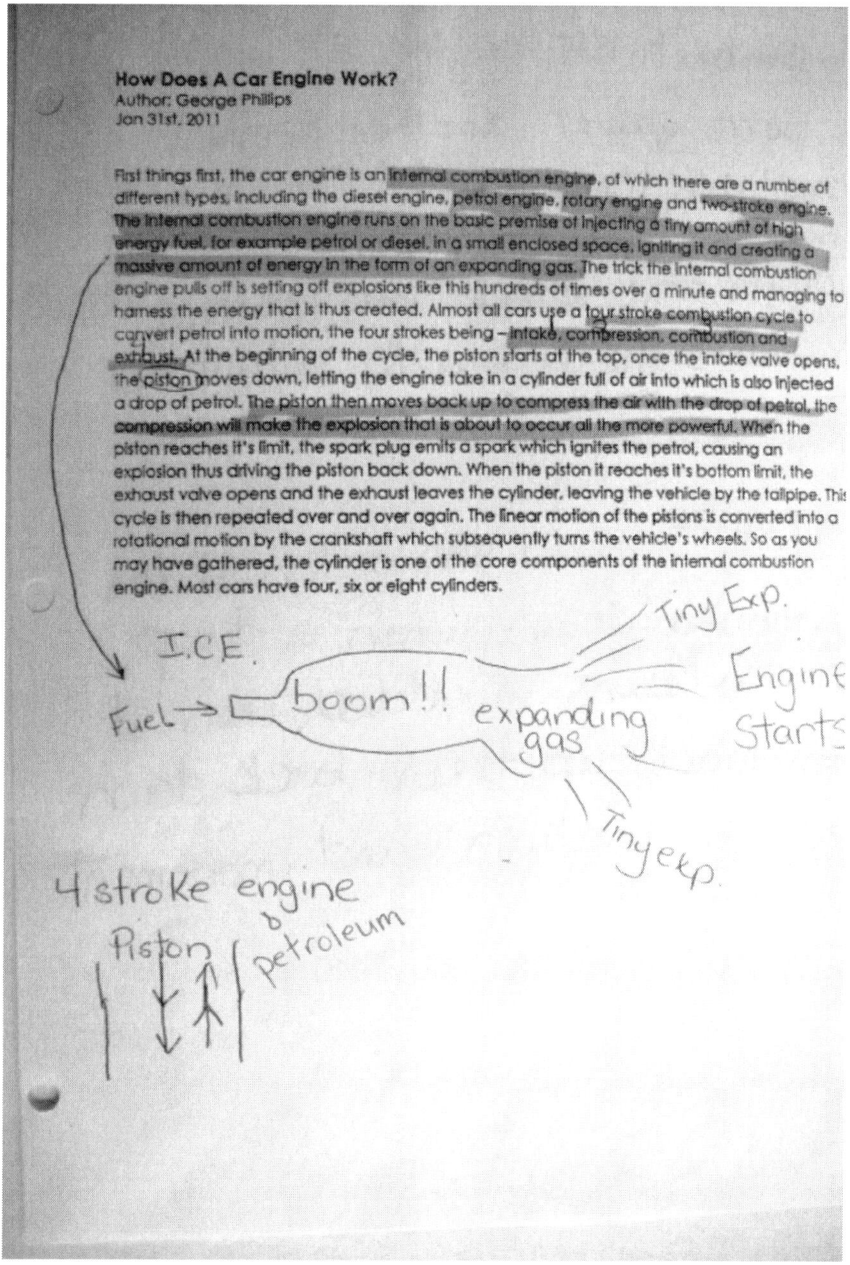

How Does A Car Engine Work?
Author: George Phillips
Jan 31st, 2011

First things first, the car engine is an internal combustion engine, of which there are a number of different types, including the diesel engine, petrol engine, rotary engine and two-stroke engine. The internal combustion engine runs on the basic premise of injecting a tiny amount of high energy fuel, for example petrol or diesel, in a small enclosed space, igniting it and creating a massive amount of energy in the form of an expanding gas. The trick the internal combustion engine pulls off is setting off explosions like this hundreds of times over a minute and managing to harness the energy that is thus created. Almost all cars use a four-stroke combustion cycle to convert petrol into motion, the four strokes being – intake, compression, combustion and exhaust. At the beginning of the cycle, the piston starts at the top, once the intake valve opens, the piston moves down, letting the engine take in a cylinder full of air into which is also injected a drop of petrol. The piston then moves back up to compress the air with the drop of petrol, the compression will make the explosion that is about to occur all the more powerful. When the piston reaches it's limit, the spark plug emits a spark which ignites the petrol, causing an explosion thus driving the piston back down. When the piston it reaches it's bottom limit, the exhaust valve opens and the exhaust leaves the cylinder, leaving the vehicle by the tailpipe. This cycle is then repeated over and over again. The linear motion of the pistons is converted into a rotational motion by the crankshaft which subsequently turns the vehicle's wheels. So as you may have gathered, the cylinder is one of the core components of the internal combustion engine. Most cars have four, six or eight cylinders.

I.C.E.

Fuel → boom!! expanding gas

Tiny Exp.

Engine Starts

Tiny exp.

4 stroke engine
Piston   petroleum

Figure 7.3.

After this, Aric displays some of his college reading students' work, showing their annotations and summaries. He reminds instructors that the thorough work they are looking at is from developmental readers, yet their annotations, visuals, and summaries are right on target. Some student samples from an actual class are included below:

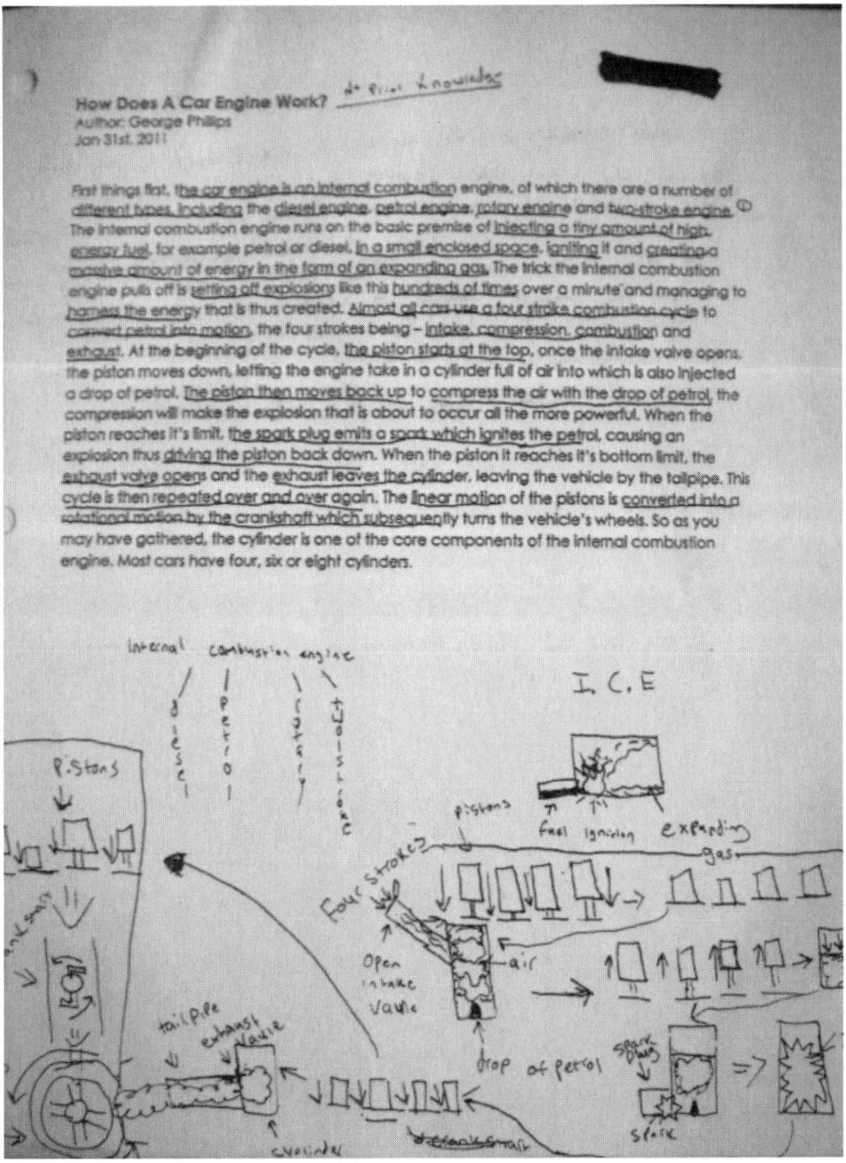

Figure 7.4.

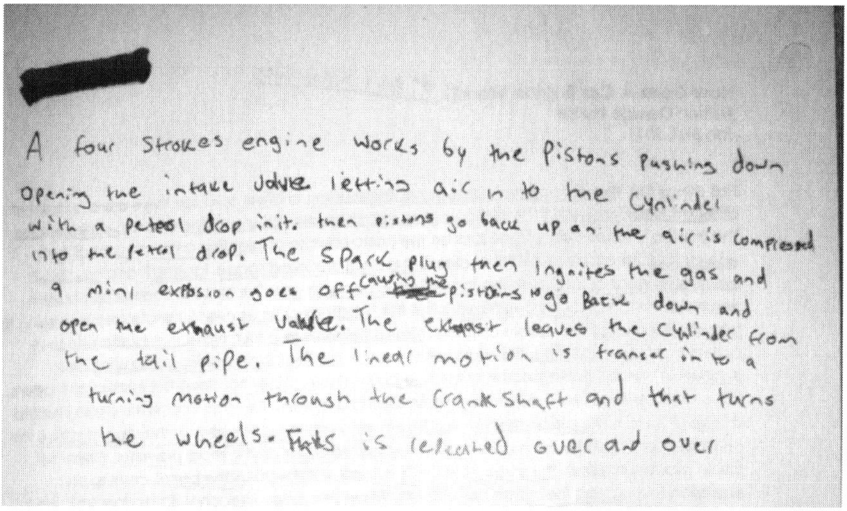

A four strokes engine works by the Pistons Pushing down Opening the intake valve letting air in to the cylinder with a petrol drop in it. then pistons go back up an the air is compressed into the petrol drop. The spark plug then ignites the gas and a mini explosion goes off. causing the pistons to go back down and open the exhaust valve. The exhaust leaves the cylinder from the tail pipe. The linear motion is transfer in to a turning motion through the crank shaft and that turns the wheels. This is repeated over and over

Figure 7.5.

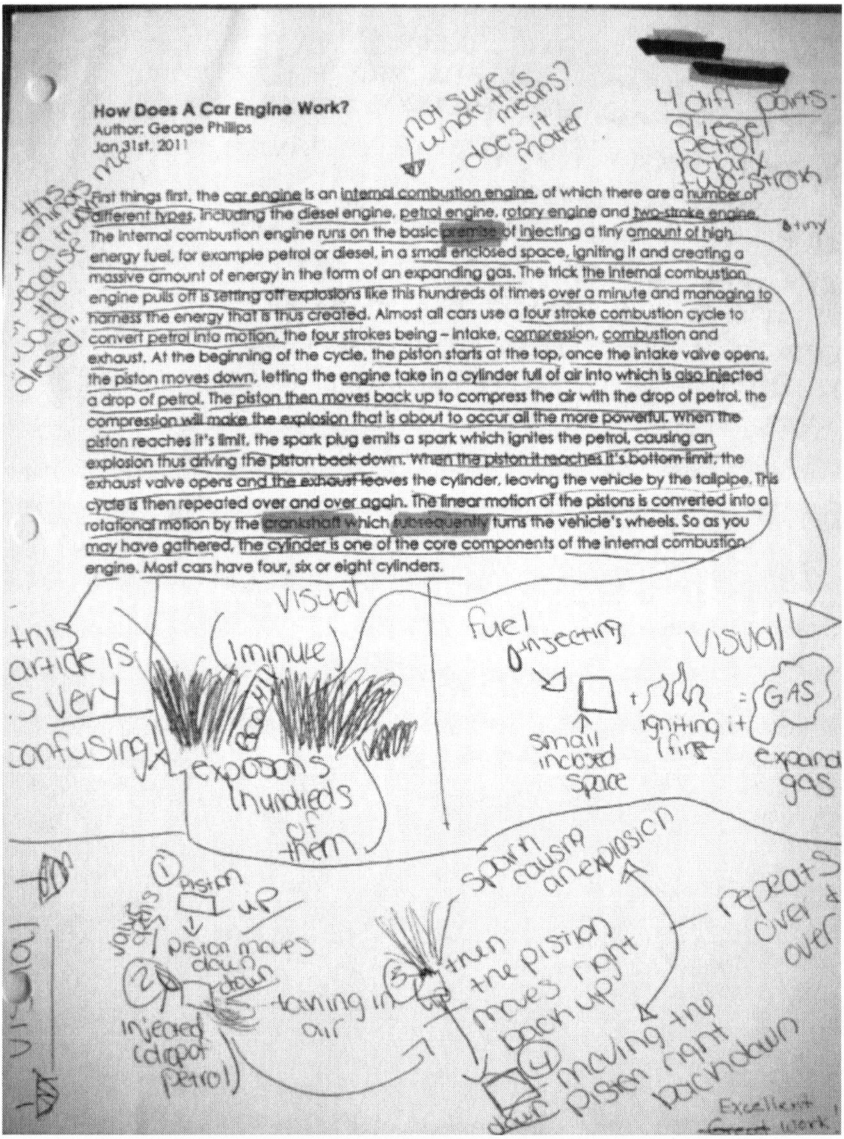

How Does A Car Engine Work?
Author: George Phillips
Jan 31st, 2011

First things first, the car engine is an internal combustion engine, of which there are a number of different types, including the diesel engine, petrol engine, rotary engine and two-stroke engine. The internal combustion engine runs on the basic premise of injecting a tiny amount of high energy fuel, for example petrol or diesel, in a small enclosed space, igniting it and creating a massive amount of energy in the form of an expanding gas. The trick the internal combustion engine pulls off is setting off explosions like this hundreds of times over a minute and managing to harness the energy that is thus created. Almost all cars use a four stroke combustion cycle to convert petrol into motion, the four strokes being – intake, compression, combustion and exhaust. At the beginning of the cycle, the piston starts at the top, once the intake valve opens, the piston moves down, letting the engine take in a cylinder full of air into which is also injected a drop of petrol. The piston then moves back up to compress the air with the drop of petrol, the compression will make the explosion that is about to occur all the more powerful. When the piston reaches it's limit, the spark plug emits a spark which ignites the petrol, causing an explosion thus driving the piston back down. When the piston it reaches it's bottom limit, the exhaust valve opens and the exhaust leaves the cylinder, leaving the vehicle by the tailpipe. This cycle is then repeated over and over again. The linear motion of the pistons is converted into a rotational motion by the crankshaft which subsequently turns the vehicle's wheels. So as you may have gathered, the cylinder is one of the core components of the internal combustion engine. Most cars have four, six or eight cylinders.

[Handwritten annotations throughout:]

not sure what this means? · does it matter

4 diff parts · diesel · petrol · rotary · two-stroke

this reminds me of a truck because the drive the diesel

tiny

this article is very confusing!

VISUAL (1 minute) explosions (hundreds of them)

fuel injecting ↓ → small inclosed space + igniting it fire = GAS expand gas

VISUAL

VISUAL

① piston up ② piston moves down — injected (drop of petrol) — taking in our

③ then spark causing an explosion — the piston moves right back up

④ moving the piston right back down

repeats over & over

Excellent! Great work!

Figure 7.6.

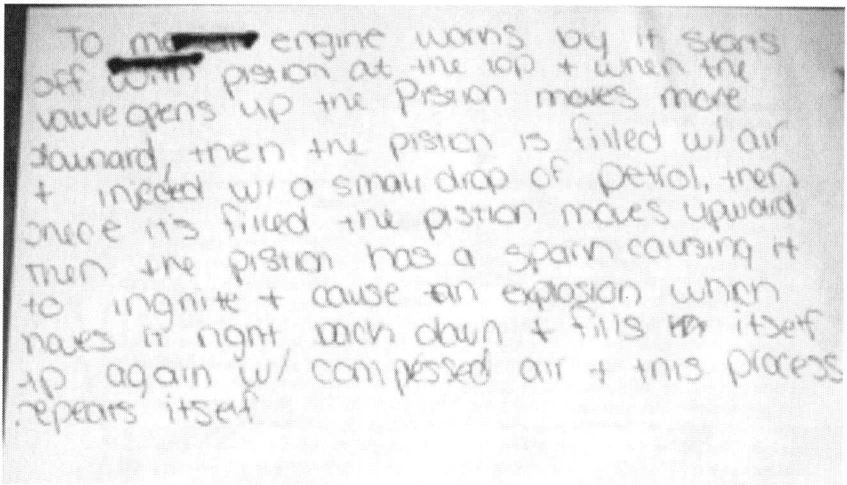

Figure 7.7.

Aric then invites the instructors to share their reactions to the activity. They all agree that creating visuals as they were reading is the reason they were able to understand how a car engine works and to describe the process so well on their own.

Below are actual survey responses from instructors who attended a faculty reading workshop on creating visuals:

What struck you during today's workshop?

- That I read something about car engines and got something out of it (I had NO idea about this stuff).
- Drawing pictures when you read. I was not able to make it through the whole article . . . but I was able to recall everything I drew.
- The power of creating visuals—what others and I were able to recall about engines after drawing representations of the information.
- How important drawing something that you don't understand can be. My comprehension came from my drawing, not just from reading.
- The technical jargon of the article and making a visual of it really surprised me as to how well this helped me remember many more details than I normally would.
- Working with visuals will be a good device to spark knowledge of content.

- Using visuals can help students retain information—especially those who are visual thinkers.

TEACHING STUDENTS TO CREATE VISUALS AS THEY READ

The best way to teach this strategy to students is through modeling and independent practice. A simple demonstration like the one described above has been proven to be very effective with students. They quickly see how creating visuals helps them to understand and remember information in a text.

It is best to use relatively short articles or excerpts because they are easier for students to get through in a classroom demonstration. Choose ones that provide easy-to-spot opportunities to create visuals, such as texts that explain a process or describe things that can be easily represented visually. Once students learn the strategy with these types of texts, they can apply them to ones that are more challenging.

Keep in mind that pictures are not the only visuals students can create. Others, such as charts, graphs, diagrams, timelines, and symbols, are also very effective to help students comprehend information and successfully recall it later.

Giving students opportunities to independently practice creating visual images is also important. Even after demonstrations that illustrate how effective this strategy can be, many students will not take time to actually try it on their own. Supplying a short passage or two for students to use as practice, either in or out of class, can act as a nudge to convince students that it might be worth their time after all.

THE BOTTOM LINE

Our students are not only surrounded by a visual society, they are immersed in it. Visuals profoundly shape how they perceive the world and how they interact with it every day. Visuals can also profoundly shape how they comprehend what they read and how they interact with a text.

A simple "car engine" demonstration will prove this. Students who can draw how a car engine works can draw how human cells divide. They can map out the Great Depression on a timeline and graph rising sea levels. They can draw the different layers of the earth's atmosphere and sketch Stonehenge. And the best part is they can better comprehend all of these things and more clearly explain them in their own words. If that's what we want our students to do, tapping in to their visual acuity just makes good sense.

TOOLBOX

- Provide students with a short list of common icons or symbols to use for annotations, such as the star symbol or thumbs ups "like" icon for something interesting, the light bulb icon for having an idea, a check mark indicating understanding, the chain link symbol for making connections, and so on. Written symbols can be used on hard copy, and electronic icons or symbols can be used on e-copy. Icon and symbol examples can be found online with a web image search.
- Charts, timelines, diagrams, tables, and graphs provide another way for students to use visuals to improve comprehension. Students often do not understand the difference between these types of visual displays. A quick search of Google Images using "visual displays of data" will provide many examples. Students can then be shown how to make simplified forms to use while annotating as they read. For students using e-texts, there are apps that allow for freehand drawing of such displays.
- Access the following resources online to show students how powerful images can be to help them learn concepts: "Learning by Drawing" by Madolyn Rogers (http://www.symmetrymagazine.org/breaking/2008/05/21/learning-by-drawing), Wrapping a Rope around the Earth Puzzle (TANTON Mathematics), "Images for Drawing to Understand Concepts" (Google Images), "Drawing to Understand Psychology" (Google Images) [note: any subject area can be typed in, such as "Drawing to Understand History," etc.].
- Use the following short excerpt, either as a classroom demonstration or for students to work on independently, to give students more practice at creating visuals as they read (full text of this article is in the appendix of chapter 3).

"Four Parenting Styles and How They Influence Child Behavior" by Kendra Cherry

The Characteristics and Effects of Parenting Styles

Authoritative Parenting

Authoritative parents have clear rules and guidelines for their kids, but they are also responsive and willing to explain the reasoning behind the rules. They listen to their kids, but are not punitive or rejecting when their children make mistakes. Baumrind suggested that these parents are supportive and monitor their children's behavior carefully in order to offer boundaries and feedback without being intrusive or restrictive.

Experts tend to agree that authoritative parenting is the overall best approach that produces children who are capable, happy, self-confident, and successful.

Authoritarian Parenting

Authoritarian parents have strict rules that they expect to be followed without question or explanation. Breaking the rules usually results in punishment. These parents expect perfect obedience and have high demands, but are not responsive to their children.

The authoritarian approach typically results in kids who are obedient, but lack self-esteem and social competence.

Permissive Parenting

Permissive parents have few rules and demands. They do not discipline their children because they have very low expectations for self-control. They do tend to be responsive to their children's needs and communicate with their kids, but they often take on a role of a friend more than that of a parent.

As a result, these children tend to have very poor self-control, often do poorly in school, and may have difficulty with authority figures.

Uninvolved Parenting

These parents provide basic survival needs for their children, but are generally very detached and offer little in terms of love, support, and communication. They make few if any demands of their children, and some may even neglect or reject their kids.

This style results in the worst outcomes across all areas including emotional, cognitive, and social development. Kids raised by uninvolved parents tend to have low social competence, low self-esteem, and poor self-regulation.

PUTTING IT TO WORK

Independent Practice for Creating Visuals

The activity described here uses a short text, "Classic Scientific Management Theory," that was included in a previous chapter to help students make connections as they read. It is also a good text to help them learn how to create visuals. It won't matter if you have already used this piece with your students. In fact, if they are somewhat familiar with the concepts in the passage, they will have an easier time using it to learn a new reading strategy.

This independent practice activity should come after an overall class demonstration of creating visuals.

Begin by giving each student a copy of the text. Then display a copy in front of the class, so students can follow along as you give instructions. Explain that they will be reading the text, stopping at each paragraph to briefly create images that will remind them of the major points being made. The idea is to be able to use their images later to write a short summary that explains the basics of "Classic Scientific Management Theory."

Illustrate by doing the first two paragraphs together. Read paragraph one, then show students that the major points are in the last sentence. Write "work processes" in the margin and draw a little test tube or a magnifying glass next to the words. Talk briefly about how this will help you remember that the theory was based on scientifically studying how work was done. Ask students what you might draw to remind you that an important aspect is to make money and cut down on waste. If they can't think of anything, help them out by drawing a dollar sign with an up arrow next to it and a small bin labeled "waste" with a large X over it.

Move on to paragraph two. This is a good opportunity to show students how to use visuals that aren't pictures. Read through the paragraph, then draw a quick timeline or graph in the margins. It would not be necessary to include all the dates, just the beginning and end and lines to show that the theory developed over time, peaked, then faded.

Stop and talk to students about how the visuals you have created so far help you remember the basic ideas about the theory presented in the first two paragraphs. Point out how you could use the images to write a short summary of those ideas.

Tell students they are to continue through the rest of the text on their own. Being asked to isolate the main points of the paragraphs will be daunting to some. Tell them to simply pick out whatever parts will help them remember basic characteristics of the theory. Go back to paragraph one and show them how the sentence you picked out contained such characteristics. Resist the temptation to help too much. Even if students seem to lack confidence, most will be able to isolate basic ideas to illustrate.

As students are working, remove your copy from the display, then go through and draw visuals on the rest of it for discussion later. For paragraph three, you might write the word "task" and draw a side-view of some stair steps and a little stick-figure labeled "manager" nearby. Paragraph four could be illustrated by a square with a smoking chimney to represent an assembly line type of factory and a short series of little connected boxes to represent workers in cubicles. To illustrate the main ideas in the final paragraph, you could write the word "organization" with a dollar sign and an up arrow next to it and draw a stick figure labeled "worker" with a crossed-out light bulb over his head.

When students are finished, go through the passage together, sharing your visuals and letting volunteers share theirs. Then have students turn their papers over and write a short summary of the basic components of "Classic Scientific Management Theory" on the back. They should not look at the text, but do this by memory based on their visual images. As they work, you should write a summary on the back of your paper too.

End by sharing your summary and letting a few students share theirs. Briefly discuss how creating visuals helped them to remember the main characteristics of the theory presented in the text.

"Classic Scientific Management Theory"

Classic scientific management theory came about in the late 1800s and has had a great impact on American business, especially manufacturing. It is called scientific because it is based on studying work processes to increase economic effectiveness and worker productivity and to decrease waste of materials, labor, and time.

The theory was initially developed in the 1880s by a man named Frederick Winslow Taylor, who began investigating labor processes of that period. Through the 1890s up to around 1910, the theory was further developed and began to have a significant impact on the manufacturing industry. Its influence peaked in the decade leading up to 1920 and then leveled out as competing theories arose. By the 1930s, the popularity of Taylor's theory had faded significantly, but its influence on industry has remained.

A main aspect of Classic Scientific Management Theory is what has become known as the division of labor, in which larger tasks are divided into smaller, more specialized ones. Individual workers perform these more specialized tasks repetitively as steps in a process to develop a product or to complete a project or work assignment. Managers closely supervise workers to ensure quality and productivity.

Factory assembly lines are an obvious example of this. However, many offices, especially bureaucracies, can be organized according to this theory with workers often in cubicles performing narrowly specified jobs overseen by various levels of management.

Whether in the factory or the office, focus tends to be on the organization as a whole rather than on the individual workers. Workers are trained to follow precise directions to complete a task. Independent thinking or decision making is not generally encouraged, nor are workers invited to give input into the company's operation. Instead, managers make decisions based on what will benefit the organization overall, such as policies that will cut costs and raise productivity levels.

PROFESSIONAL SPOTLIGHT READING INTERVIEW
WITH BRIAN AMSDEN

Title: Electrical Manufacturing Sales Representative
Location: Cleveland, Ohio

Amelia: Can you describe the reading demands in your profession?

Brian: In electrical manufacturing, there are always new products. Also, about half of our business is energy savings. That industry is changing every day. So, really what I'm reading constantly is what we call product bulletins. Manufacturers are different. If I have twenty manufacturers, some are more progressive and come out with more new products. I have one who comes out with a new product every eight weeks. So every eight weeks, there is something new for a salesman or sales organization. We have an organization of twenty-six people right now. So for us, it's great to have new products, something to be out in the street with. So we're constantly reading product bulletins and feature benefit statements. Some of our stuff is very technical, like the tools electricians are using or the newest energy-saving lights.

Amelia: Are these things you need to read usually online or in hard copy?

Brian: We get our first releases over the Internet—e-mails, bulletins. It's faster. But we'll generally still get hard copies as well.

Amelia: If students graduate from college and they want to work in your type of profession, can they make it if they're not proficient readers?

Brian: The new product information is the majority of what we're reading, but it's also e-mails. They are just unbelievable now, the quantity. No, people in this profession really couldn't make it easily if they couldn't read. Could they just get by? Maybe. But they would not be very successful.

Amelia: It sounds like the reading in your profession requires you to take it in and really comprehend information.

Brian: Yes, definitely. Reading in my profession requires a lot of comprehension. You then have to take that information to become a resource to your customers, to get that information into their hands, to explain it, to demonstrate it.

Amelia: How did you learn to be a proficient reader? Did you go to a great elementary school or did your parents push it at home, or did you learn it on the job, especially with that technical reading?

Brian: A lot of the technical stuff was hands-on. I was fortunate enough to start in the industry young, right out of college. That's all I've ever done. Some guys in the industry have gone the technical electrician route. They've been electricians before and then moved into our sales field, which has helped them. But for me, I went a different route. I went to the university, and then I was able to get a lot of hands-on training, which is nice. We have a wide range of products. Some are very technical and some are more basic, but for technical stuff, hands-on helps. Then we read about it later and rely on those experiences to understand it.

Amelia: When you look back at your college experience, is there anything you know now about reading that you wish you had known then?

Brian: Yeah. Applying and thinking about that lesson or that reading assignment and really getting the actual ideas out of it. Then, understanding that sometimes we act on the ideas now and sometimes we put them away in our memory banks. The information is available, but it's not needed yet. I didn't know then that some things I read I needed to act on and some I needed to learn for use later. When I read now, I do both of those things.

Amelia: So when you read information, do you think, "Okay, this is something I have to use right now and this is something I'm going to need later"?

Brian: Yes. I fortunately have good recall and can remember where I read something and when, and I can file things in my mind effectively. That happens a lot, especially with the energy saving and the lighting. A lot of technology moves very fast. Some things aren't ready for the public yet. Then when things are set and the manufacturer gets the price points ready, then you can use what you learned to get that out to the market.

APPENDIX

How Does A Car Engine Work?

Author: George Phillips

January 31, 2011

First things first, the car engine is an internal combustion engine, of which there are a number of different types, including the diesel engine, petrol engine, rotary engine and two-stroke engine. The internal combustion engine runs on the basic premise of injecting a tiny amount of high energy fuel, for example petrol or diesel, in a small enclosed space, igniting it and creating a massive amount of energy in the form of an expanding gas. The trick the internal combustion engine pulls off is setting off explosions like this hundreds of times over a minute and managing to harness the energy that is thus created. Almost all cars use a four stroke combustion cycle to convert petrol into motion, the four strokes being—intake, compression, combustion and exhaust. At the beginning of the cycle, the piston starts at the top, once the intake valve opens, the piston moves down, letting the engine take in a cylinder full of air into which is also injected a drop of petrol. The piston then moves back up to compress the air with the drop of petrol, the compression will make the explosion that is about to occur all the more powerful. When the piston reaches its limit, the spark plug emits a spark which ignites the petrol, causing an explosion thus driving the piston back down. When the piston reaches its bottom limit, the exhaust valve opens and the exhaust leaves the cylinder, leaving the vehicle by the tailpipe. This cycle is then repeated over and over again. The linear motion of the pistons is converted into a rotational motion by the crankshaft which subsequently turns the vehicle's wheels. So as you may have gathered, the cylinder is one of the core components of the internal combustion engine. Most cars have four, six or eight cylinders.

8

Keeping It Real

Education is not the learning of facts, but the training of the mind to think.

—Albert Einstein

Professional Spotlight

Figure 8.1.

I had to listen in class, write down notes, then read them into the tape recorder, and then take those questions at the end of the book and answer them the best I could. I'd have to keep skimming back in the book and try to find the answers. But I got in the habit of reading.

Kenneth Seel,
Marriage and Family Therapist &
Certified Alcohol and Drug Counselor

Chapter 8

Reasonable question: Will teaching reading strategies in my content area really have enough impact on students to make it worth the time and effort?

In faculty workshops, instructors rarely raise an eyebrow when shown statistics about how many students enter college unprepared for the challenges of academic reading. They've seen the blank looks when they ask questions about an article they assigned their students to read. They've graded the exams that show how little students understand about key concepts in their textbooks. And they believe that students are generally telling the truth when they say they did the reading but just didn't understand it.

What these instructors do question, however, is if teaching reading strategies in their classes will make any significant difference. They want to know it's really worth the sacrifice of valuable class time that could be spent teaching course content.

DOES TEACHING READING STRATEGIES REALLY CHANGE ANYTHING?

Some of the best proof comes straight from the mouths of students. Below are some actual survey responses that represent what they say over and over about the benefits of learning reading strategies:

- I have learned how to underline properly now. Before I would underline just about everything because I would think it's all important and I liked seeing that I did a little bit of work. Safe to say I now know the difference between underlining (highlighting) what's important and what I just like to see to make myself feel better.
- One of the things I will take throughout my education (career) is the reading strategies. One of the ones I will use most is crossing out information that is not needed. I never truly applied this to anything until this year and it has helped a lot even with my math class. Ever since I learned to cross out things that do not matter I have used it on all of my math work and it has really helped me pass the tests because before I would read the problem and not know where to start, but now I know what to cross out and I can get straight to the problem. The teacher has even told me that she likes how I solve the story problems. She said, "It seems like you understand them more now."

- Reading is the only one thing that I really struggled with all my life but now I just go back and look at my purpose.
- When you began to teach us how to annotate the text, that's when I started to improve my reading and comprehension.
- Reading science textbooks has always been difficult for me. The vocabulary can be challenging. The content can be dry and the chapters can be very long. Using the reading strategies I am now able to determine what's important about the section and what the focus of the chapter is by seeking out the main ideas and focusing on key words, which are often displayed in boldface type. Applying this strategy will help cut down the time it takes me to read the chapter. Using the active reading strategy of always reading with a pen or pencil and pad of paper will remind me to continually make notes and ask more questions about what I am reading to ensure I am pulling out the needed information as well as understanding the information.
- One thing I am already using in my other classes is the active reading skills. I always find myself making sure I have a pen or pencil to mark the text in many different ways.
- One of my friends was actually struggling with reading larger pieces of text and I showed her a little bit of what we learned in this class and it helped her a lot. The other day we were studying together and I saw her use it almost the entire time.

It is obvious from these responses, and so many others like them, that students understand the impact of learning reading strategies. They know they have turned a corner and are moving toward being more competent readers, and they know it's because they landed in a classroom where an instructor took time to teach them pivotal reading skills.

HOW MUCH TIME DOES IT REALLY TAKE?

The truth is teaching reading strategies will take time, especially when you first get started. There will be an initial learning curve to get familiar with the strategies to decide which are most needed in your content area. For instance, a biology instructor might decide to choose strategies that help students learn specialized vocabulary. A history instructor might focus instead on teaching students to ask questions as they read.

Time will also be needed up front to prepare short lessons and activities. Detailed lessons, descriptions of suggested activities, and lists of resources have been included in this book to help with this. Many of these can be pulled out and used with very little preparation. Also, once teaching material is put together, it can be used multiple times with other classes without a lot of extra work.

When it comes to actual teaching time, you might need around thirty minutes of a few class periods, especially early in a semester, to introduce students to the concept of active reading and to demonstrate some key strategies. After that, you could use ten- to fifteen-minute mini-lessons spread out over the course of the semester to quickly model new strategies or to allow students to practice ones they have previously learned.

All of this might seem like quite a sacrifice in an already crowded semester, and it is. However, it's a sacrifice worth making. First, students who are equipped with strategies often view academic reading as more manageable. When this happens, the likelihood they will actually read the texts you assign goes up. That's a big deal. Those texts are important to your content area. If they weren't, you wouldn't have assigned them. The more reading students do, the better.

Second, students who are equipped with strategies are more likely to comprehend what they read. That's also a big deal. The goal of any college class is for students to learn. When comprehension goes up, learning goes up. This actually helps the time issue to even out. Once students begin to read with more understanding, not as much time needs to be spent explaining and reexplaining concepts. Class discussions are more productive, and less time is used reviewing for quizzes and tests.

MAKING THE MOST OF TEACHING TIME

There are three words to keep in mind when it comes to teaching reading strategies in content area classes: *early*, *frequent*, and *fast*. Begin as early in a semester as you can. The sooner you get students started, the sooner their reading comprehension will improve. Students will also have more chances to practice using various strategies with you there to help them along.

Work in teaching reading strategies as frequently as you can. Repetition will strengthen and cement students' skills. Also, the more often you focus students on learning to be effective readers, the more they will see it as important. Once students buy in to the value of reading strategies, they will be more intentional about using them.

Not only should reading lessons be frequent; they should be fast. It is well known that teaching new information in short bursts over a period of time is more effective than teaching it in one or two long sessions. Likewise, it is better to teach reading strategies several times during a semester for ten to fifteen minutes than to teach once or twice for hours at a time.

Another way to make the most of teaching time is to use content-area texts for reading strategy demonstrations and practice. This allows instructors to teach subject-area content and reading strategies at the same time.

Also, since you are the expert in your field, students will greatly benefit from seeing how you navigate content-specific texts, think through material, and apply reading strategies that can save time and increase comprehension and recall. Students will learn by watching you determine what's important enough to read (and *why* it's important), what can be scanned and what can be skipped, and what you find important enough to bullet, so it can be remembered and used later.

A resource called "Take Ten" was included in chapter one. For easy reference, it is included in the appendix of this chapter as well. It contains ideas for embedding reading strategies into content-area lessons in as little as ten minutes. These types of activities can be done weekly with very little interruption of normal class procedures.

Including accountability is another time consideration. Why waste time teaching reading strategies if students aren't going to use them? As mentioned earlier in the book, most students don't do optional. Even those who have bought in and understand how vital it is to be an effective reader will be less likely to apply the strategies in meaningful ways unless there is some sort of accountability attached.

For most instructors, keeping students accountable is code for "grading." Not necessarily so with reading strategies. Simply roaming around the classroom checking students' texts for annotations or asking students to forward pictures of marked-up pages to the instructor will keep students accountable without requiring extra grading.

The class time used to teach reading strategies will be better spent if students actually use what they learn. Built-in accountability is one way to get them to do this.

THE BOTTOM LINE

Instructors know that not being able to read with comprehension is a major roadblock to learning. And they will get on board to help the struggling readers in their classes if they are given effective tools that are worth the time and effort it will take to use them. Instructors don't need fads or trends. They need solid, proven techniques that work. The reading strategies described in *Help! My College Students Can't Read* are such techniques. They are relatively simple to teach and can be embedded into class instruction in practical ways that do not compromise the integrity of content-area courses.

Most important of all, these strategies really do help students be more effective readers who can think their way through content-area texts, more clearly comprehend the information they find there, and more effectively learn and use that information. This is what college instructors care about the most. For them, this is the real bottom line.

PROFESSIONAL SPOTLIGHT READING INTERVIEW WITH KENNETH SEEL

Title: Marriage and Family Therapist & Certified Alcohol and Drug Counselor
Location: Jackson, Michigan

Amelia: Could you talk about your experiences with reading?

Ken: I was a very, very poor student in school. I got the reputation that I was one of the dummies. They just passed that along as I went through school. When I graduated from high school, I was going to join the military, but it was the Vietnam War, and a friend of mine, actually the father of the lady I was dating, suggested that probably was not a good idea, people getting killed and whatnot. He encouraged me to go to junior college. I thought, "I'll never go to junior college. I graduated with a D average," but he told me he could help me get in.

My biggest problem was I couldn't read. When they tested me, I actually read at about a fourth-grade level. I basically couldn't read at all. Since I enjoyed sailing and scuba diving and things like that, this man found magazines and books like that, things that interested me, and he got me to read them. That's how I got started reading. Then, he also gave me storybooks and paperback books to read.

He also told me what to do when I was in class. One was taking very copious notes, and then at the end of every chapter of every book, they would always have something like twenty questions of things you needed to know. I'd answer all those questions, and then I tape recorded everything. That's how I studied. Everything I had, all my studying, was done on tape. I even carried that through when I went into grad school years later. All my notes, everything that I had to study, I always put it on tape. Because when I listened to it, I could get it better than when I read it.

Amelia: Were you actually reading the text aloud into the tape recorder and then listening to it later?

Ken: No. I'd read the book, but especially in junior college it was very difficult to understand things I was reading. I had to listen in class, write down notes, then read them into the tape recorder, and then take those questions at the end of the book and answer them the best I could. I'd have to keep skimming back in the book and try to find the answers. But I got into the habit of reading.

Later, I lived in the Caribbean for years and there wasn't TV, and I lived on boats a lot. The only recreation I had was reading. So to this day, I always have two books going constantly. I'll have some junk novel I'm reading but also some psychology book or something, and I read every night before I go to bed. When I'm hanging out at the house, that's what I do, I read a lot.

Amelia: So, actually the more reading you did the better you got at it?

Ken: That's how I learned to read, by reading.

Amelia: How much reading do you think is required in your type of profession as an alcohol and drug counselor?

Ken: Every day when I teach groups, they have process notes they fill out. I have to read those and make my notes. So, there's a lot of reading and writing. We do assessments. So I sit down and talk to people, and I have to type the information about their history. So, there's a lot to do. There's a lot of reading. And then, any information about any new idea or new technique or just basic information about the drug and alcohol field or psychology field is found in books. You have to read it and read articles.

Amelia: If you could estimate in percentages, how much of the reading material you look at is online vs. hard copy?

Ken: Most of it is books. Now, when it comes to work-related material, probably about half and half. When it comes to recreational reading, I still like books.

Amelia: If you were thinking about people who were fresh out of college, what kinds of challenges do you think they might encounter going into your field if they were struggling readers?

Ken: Well, there's a lot of paperwork to do when you're in this business. It takes up a good deal of time. And, if you have problems reading, it's just going to slow you down. Every time I teach a class with fourteen or fifteen people in it, at the end of that class I have to read their progress notes and write my assessments. There's a lot of paperwork to be done, and if you're a slow reader or have difficulty reading, it can be a problem.

Amelia: When you say "class" you mean groups of incarcerated people who are taking classes you conduct?

Ken: Yes, I facilitate groups whether they're process groups or didactic groups. The point is that when you're done with these groups, there are notes to be written and forms to be filled out, and it takes a lot of time. If you're a poor reader, it's going to get in the way.

APPENDIX

Take Ten

Take Ten Minutes to Embed Reading Strategies into Each Class.

- When handing out articles/texts, ask students to write a **prediction** (guess) at the top of the page indicating what the text will be about based on the title. This will access prior knowledge.

- When handing out articles/texts, ask students to write their **purpose** for reading (reason for reading/what they think the author wants them to know) at the top of the page. If students know what they're looking for, their brains will help them find it.
- Ask students to write their **questions** in the margins as they read. At the end of class, use the last ten minutes for students to share their questions aloud. Others might be able to provide the answers. This will encourage students to be aware of their questions, to clarify them, and to search for answers as they read.
- Ask students to write **connections** to the text in the margins as they read. At the end of class, use the last ten minutes for students to share their connections aloud or in writing and discuss how their connections helped them construct meaning within the text.
- Ask students to cross out any unnecessary information as they read. This will create the potential for more focused reading by helping them to **determine what's important** and by keeping extraneous material from muddying the waters as they think through the text.
- Each time you assign a chapter, show your students (using the doc cam and text) what you would pay attention to in the text and what you might **read, scan or skip.**
- Choose an important paragraph (or even just four or five sentences) to read aloud, and then **jot down** a couple of bullet points of things you find important in the passage and why.

Here's the beauty of it all: Take Ten is a small time investment that yields huge payoffs. You teach your students to be more effective readers with no extra prep and no extra grading. Simply present the task and then place check marks at the tops of students' work as you roam around the room to keep them focused and accountable.

References

Alexander, M. 2010. *The New Jim Crow: Mass Incarceration in the Age of Colorblindness*. New York: New Press.

Brown, W., and R. Brown. 2011. *Print Reading for Industry*. 9th ed. Tinley Park, IL: Goodheart-Willcox.

Daniels, H., and N. Steineke. 2011. *Text and Lessons for Content-Area Reading.* Portsmouth, NH: Heinemann.

Di Tommaso, K. "Strategies to Facilitate Reading Comprehension among College Transition Students." n.d. http://www.collegetransition.org/promising practices.research.readingstrategies.html.

Fisher, D., and N. Frey. 2012. *Improving Adolescent Literacy: Content Area Strategies at Work*. Boston: Pearson.

Fremgen, B. F. 2012. *Medical Law and Ethics*. 4th ed. Upper Saddle River, NJ: Pearson.

Galeano, E. 1989. "Celebration of the Human Voice/2." In *The Book of Embraces*, translated by C. Belfrage. New York: Norton. http://teaching.quotidiana.org/soe/humanvoice2/index.html.

Gilroy, S. 2004. "Interrogating Texts: 6 Reading Habits to Develop in Your First Year at Harvard." Harvard College Library, August 25. isites.harvard.edu/fs/docs/icb.topic33378.files/interrogatingtexts.pdf.

Handy, T., and M. Stein. 2010. "Teaching Academic Reading Strategies to Improve Learning." http://www.nwfsc.edu/sacs/focus%20documents/qep-09102010.pdf.

Harvey, S., and A. Goudvis. 2007. *Strategies that Work: Teaching Comprehension for Understanding and Engagement*. 2nd ed. Portland, ME: Stenhouse.

Humes, H. 1993. "The Cough." In *Microfiction: An Anthology of Really Short Stories*, edited by J. Stern, 26–27. http://books.google.com.

Hurst, B., and C. J. Pearman. n.d. "Teach Reading? But I'm Not a Reading Teacher!" http://education.missouristate.edu/assets/AcadEd/Hurst_Pearman .pdf.

Karp, H. 2010. "The NBA Locker-Room Nerds: International Players Are Helping to Bring Back an Erstwhile League Pastime." *Wall Street Journal*, February 10. http://online.wsj.com/article/SB10001424052748704140104575057521488502914.html.

Keene, E. O., and S. Zimmermann. 1997. *Mosiac of Thought: Teaching Comprehension in a Reader's Workshop.* Portsmouth, NH: Heinemann.

Konnikova, M. 2012. "On Writing, Memory, and Forgetting: Socrates and Hemingway Take on Zeigarnik." *Scientific American*, April 30. http://blogs .scientificamerican.com/literally-psyched/2012/04/30/on-writing-memory-and -forgetting-socrates-and-hemingway-take-on-zeigarnik/.

Kouyoumdjian, H. 2012. "Learning through Visuals: Visual Imagery in the Classroom." *Psychology Today*, July 20. http://www.psychologytoday.com/ blog/get-psyched/201207/learning-through-visuals.

Lewin, L. 2010. "Teaching Critical Reading with Questioning Strategies." *Educational Leadership* 67 (6). http://www.ascd.org/publications/educational-leadership/ mar10/vol67/num06/Teaching-Critical-Reading-with-Questioning-Strategies .aspx.

Lickerman, A. 2009. "How to Remember Things: Proven Strategies to Improve Your Memory." *Psychology Today*, November 16. http://www.psychology today.com/blog/ happiness-in-world/200911/how-remember-things.

Nakamura, B. 2012. "Editorial: 16 Is Too Young to Quit School in New Economy." *USA Today*, February 16. http://usatoday30.usatoday.com/news/ opinion/editorials/story/2012-02-14/dropout-high-school-16-18/53096824/1.

Pichert, J. W., and R. C. Anderson. 1977. "The House: In Taking Different Perspectives on a Story." *Journal of Educational Psychology* 69: 309–15.

Robbins, A. n.d. "How to Have Self-Confidence." http://www.youtube.com/ watch?v=tUShaG9ygBM.

Shortt, Russell. 2009. "How Does a Car Engine Work?" *Articlesbase*, March 2. http://www.articlesbase.com/science-articles/how-does-a-car-engine-work -796816.html.

Test Your Awareness: Do the Test. n.d. https:// www.youtube.com/watch?v =Ah g6qcgoay4.

Tovani, C. 2000. *I Read It, But I Don't Get It: Comprehension Strategies for Adolescent Readers*. Portland, ME: Stenhouse.

Tucker, I. B. 2011. *Economics for Today*. 7th ed. Mason, OH: South-Western Cengage Learning.

University of Alabama. "How to Improve Your Reading Skills." n.d. http://www.ctl.ua.edu/ctlstudyaids/studyskillsflyers/reading/improvereadingskills.htm.

University of Michigan. "Strategies to Use While You Are Reading." n.d. http://www.lsa.umich.edu/advising/academicsupport/strategiesforsuccess/readingforcollege/strategiestousewhileyouarereading.

About the Author

Amelia Leighton Gamel is Lead Faculty for the reading program at Jackson College in Michigan and was the recipient of the 2014 J. Ward Preston Outstanding Faculty Award. She also serves as a facilitator for campus-wide reading workshops and classroom demonstrations in all content areas and works closely with high school teachers to implement school-wide reading initiatives. Amelia holds an MA in Education from Spring Arbor University and has fifteen years of experience in education as a reading specialist, college faculty member and administrator, educational presenter, and public school teacher. Amelia's passion lies in helping at-risk students. She has a special interest in research and techniques that promote the academic success and advancement of African American males.